The Art of Composure

A Beginners Guide to Performing Under Pressure in Communication, Conflict, High-Stakes Environments, Problem-Solving and Leadership.

Andrew Hudson

Table of Contents

Introduction

If I look back at my life today, I can see how selling myself short like a desperate door-to-door salesman, always stumbling over his words and having no sales to show for his efforts, was of no consequence. No one was buying into how I used to project myself. No one was listening, and I doubt if anyone was even interested. As a young man, I honestly believed that I wouldn't amount to anything in life. I didn't know it at the time, but simply put, I lacked composure. I lacked self-confidence and I was always anxious about what the next day would bring.

The day that passed had, of course, brought me nothing. Or so I thought. Back then, I could not have known. Lacking composure and self-confidence, I was far too distracted to know any better and was always worrying about things I had no control over. Back then, it would not have mattered if I simply focused on the things that I could do. It would have helped if I had adopted a more positive posture and mindset that could have helped me to not only do the things that I could conceivably do but do the things that needed to be done to help me get by, and who knows, actually do things that I wanted to do.

But no, I had no idea what I wanted to do. I always seemed to be too busy watching what others were doing. Instead of using them as a positive example of what could be achieved, I kept asking myself: Why not me? Why can't I do what they're doing? Why can't I have what they have? Girlfriends, fast cars, money to show for my efforts, but what efforts? Until I saw the light, these negative preoccupations continued to distress me while I spent more time than I should have watching other young men I used to socialize with, down at the gym and elsewhere, leave their turf and go on to seek and find greener pastures.

I wasn't jealous of them. It's just that I wanted to do things that I thought I couldn't do. I wanted to do things that other guys were already doing before the age of 21, like driving a fancy car or going to grad school, but I couldn't seem to do it myself. But thankfully, like you will do in the days and weeks to come, I turned the corner.

I realized one day that my life was running away from me while I drifted from one dead-end job to the next. I realized that I was the only one who could stop myself from sinking in the windswept drift sands of life. While I continued to carry interests which vaguely piqued me, there was one pursuit that gave me more passion than anything else, perhaps even life itself. I lived, ate, and breathed boxing.

So, one day, after punching away my frustrations on the punching bag in a quiet corner of the noisy, crowded gym, I finally stepped affirmatively into the ring of life. I was nervous as a butterfly, and already, I had an ominous feeling that if I was to become a full-fledged boxer, I would emerge from my corner without any threatening notion of a sting. Even so, I was in my element, even if for a few universal moments, and despite being beaten to a pulp. Figuratively speaking of course. Losing fight after fight, suffering only a few bruises here and there from opponents I could conceivably have beaten, it was my self-loathing ego that had got the better of me. And in those rare moments that I was able to shuffle my way to the middle of the ring to face the music and another round of well-timed punches, I remained toneless.

What We Know About Being Composed

I always seemed to freeze during moments when it mattered most. Crowds outside the ring, baying for blood, had nothing to do with it. Losing fight after fight, never able to compose myself, I came to accept that I had no aptitude for hardcore prizefighting in front of a sweaty audience. Lacking composure, I couldn't communicate with my fists.

I wasn't the only one. In the years after my positive transformation, also learning to accept my limitations, I continued to make time for the gym after work. Initially, it was a good way to keep fit and my frustrations and fear of failing in life at bay. Doing that, I watched many young men pass through those doors, low in self-esteem, just like I was back in the day. I could relate to what they were going through, and I wanted to help them. Today, I want to help you too. I want to help you get off the floor of the ring of life, and make something of your life.

Components of Composure

Of course, at this stage of your reading, we can agree that it's easier said than done. But while you gather your thoughts, let me explain how this book will help you. After I've exposed you to the harsh reality of what a lack of composure does to a man, I'll start introducing new strategies that'll help you start your transition from being what others have called a born loser to a fully composed, well-rounded gentleman, oozing confidence in the ring or the workplace, and on the dating scene. In the meantime, make a note in your journal (yes, go get yourself an exercise book to take notes and compose your thoughts) that there are three core components of composure that you'll be introduced to in this book: emotional regulation, self-control, and cognitive clarity.

This is how it works: When you're composed, confident in your abilities and how you're feeling in the moment, even self-indulgent in a guilt-free way, you're able to communicate your actions and intentions in a way that only you can understand. This has something to do with your ability to accept who you are as a unique individual, always prepared to plaster emotional bruises if and when they occur, and patiently give them time to heal while you get on with your life. And if you're able to do that, others will know your intentions too.

Emotional Regulation

When you're composed, you're sure of yourself, not cocksure and overconfident but confident in your abilities and the way you project yourself toward others. In the ring of life, your opponents will note that you're no pushover. They're left with no alternative but to take more time in their corner to size you up. If you're in control of your emotions, you won't be falling for any attempts on their part to mislead you and force you into making a mistake.

They're none the wiser when you're able to regulate your emotions as well. It's almost like playing a game of poker. Your opponents have no idea what cards you're holding because of your ability to hide your emotions. While they cannot know what you're thinking, your ability to mask your emotions and intentions allows you to be in full control of your destiny.

Self-Control

But in order to be in full control of your emotions, you still need to exercise self-control. Apart from being able to discipline yourself, this concept allows you to respond appropriately to the ongoing demands of daily life that you're faced with. Holding all the best cards in the deck, you're in control of a repertoire of emotions that allow you to be flexible while responding to social expectations. Holding all the best cards in the deck is not a stroke of good luck because it takes time and practice to master the arts of composure. And it takes discipline too.

When you're in control of your emotions, you'll also be able to delay spontaneous outbursts which leave little to the imagination of your opponents. You won't be prone to angry outbursts outside the ring either. Rather, and if it comes to that, you'll take out your frustrations on the punching bag. Figuratively speaking of course, but no harm in hitting the punching bag down at your local gym. It's good exercise for your upper body, as well as your calves and thighs. In this book, you'll learn that it's okay to have guilt-free motions of anger. It's just a question of controlling it.

Finally, in the context of this book's motivational message, executive functions don't have anything to do with boardroom swindles or business management acumen. It doesn't have anything to do with managing a group of novices down at the gym either. Rather, executive functions, of which self-control as a form of inhibitory control is an important part, contribute toward the effective day-to-day management of your life, alongside helping you to achieve your goals, when properly carried out.

Cognitive Clarity

Cognitive clarity, on the other hand, is something I only came across recently during one of my regular sessions of reading into all things psychological. Personally, I regard my mental ability as a reflection of my acquired cognitive clarity which takes time, practice, and discipline to develop, just like self-control. Over time, you'll be able to remember things more easily, even when you're stressed, think quickly on your feet, and even reserve judgment for those who don't always see eye to eye with you.

Just like our muscles, our mental abilities need ongoing training and exercise to allow us to remain mentally fit, bearing in mind that mental clarity is not, nor never will be, a given. Make a note in your journal that this is something you're going to have to work on throughout your life: Work toward improving your mental abilities without being overwhelmed by a life that will never be without its challenges. The work you do today will stand you in good stead to enjoy a healthy, productive, and engaged life long into the future. For the time being, don't worry too much about the meaning behind the above introductions because I'll be expanding on these later in the book.

What It Feels Like to Be Under Pressure

In the meantime, we still have to deal with the daily pressures of life. At this stage, I don't think I need to tell you what it really feels like because it's something you're dealing with right now. So that you have something to think about later on when you work your way through some of my suggestions, make a few more notes in your journal about what it feels like to crack under pressure.

How This Book Will Benefit You

Before I pick up from where I left off at the beginning of the Introduction, let me tell you a bit about how this book will benefit you. To motivate you to successfully and purposefully complete your reading of this book, I've linked composure to the following four areas of life that I'm sure you're quite familiar with by now:

- **Daily Life**: When you have composure, life won't control you. You'll control life. You'll also be able to overcome your anxiety issues, manage stressful situations more effectively, and improve your self-esteem.

- **How You Communicate**: When you have composure, you won't freeze. Rather, you'll be able to overcome your social anxiety issues and enjoy socializing with others. You'll build new relationships, ones that you'll want to keep. And while others will get what you're trying to communicate, you'll have time to attract women and do so with confidence.

- **Dealing With Conflict**: When you have composure, you won't cower or run a mile. You'll learn to avoid violent situations and prevent problems from running away from you. And while you improve your relationships with yourself and those who matter to you, you'll be able to beat those who continue to be hell-bent on destroying you.

- **Dealing With High-Stakes Environments**: The ability to deal with such situations requires composure, and when you have it by the bucket load, your improved confidence levels will empower you to be better at solving problems, be more efficient and productive in the workplace with a better reputation, have that competitive advantage over your opponent in a sporting events, or ace your term papers if you're still at school.

Over time, you'll have a positive impact on others. You'll become a leader or a great role model for them to follow. Once you start achieving results, you'll be successful in life.

My Story So Far

Before I finish my Introduction to *The Art of Composure,* let me tell you a bit more about myself. Before I started taking my interest in psychology seriously with regular reading, I took up mentoring new boxers down at the local gym. Today, while I still deliver my hours of coaching to recruits who've come through the ranks at our downtown gym, I seem to spend more time writing. Today, I'm an author of books that focus on developing the mental strength of my readers.

My work doesn't focus on boxers and other sportsmen. If you've never exercised a day in your life (and I recommend that you give this some serious thought today), you'll still gain mental strength and motivation from reading this and other books that I've produced. You don't need to get in the ring and expose yourself to a barrage of punches or run the NYC marathon to crack the four-hour mark to derive maximum benefit from practicing the suggestions that my book provides and to enjoy the benefits I listed earlier.

Moreover, this book is designed to serve the purposes and interests of guys from all walks of life, whether you're psyching yourself to be a work-from-home stockbroker or just a regular guy who wants to enjoy life to the fullest without having to endure more hang-ups than are necessary. I can relate to being regular. After all, I'm still at heart a regular guy, just like you.

The Confidence Workbook

A hands-on guide containing 7 simple strategies designed to help you build self-esteem and develop confidence today.

Follow this link to get your **free** online copy

subscribepage.io/buildconfidence

1. Understanding Composure

In the Introduction, I pointed out that there were at least three psychological components required for composure to be achieved. In this chapter, I will be going further than the introductions I provided to emotional regulation, self-control, and cognitive clarity, by providing more in-depth descriptions. But before we get that far, we need to debunk some of the misconceptions attached to composure. This, to my mind, will help you to broaden your understanding of composure as a psychological tool that needs to be utilized by you at all times of the day.

I also need to provide you with something of a scene-setter to warm you up to just how significant composure is for all aspects of your life. In this case, let me introduce you to two real-life people who, as it turns out, could not be more different from each other. For instance, if you asked my elderly father who Eminem was, the usually self-assured and knowledgeable gentleman would look at you with a vacant expression in his eyes, not knowing who the heck you were talking about.

Perhaps you know more about the life and times of the American rap star and actor Eminem than I do, perhaps not. All I'm doing is showcasing aspects of this man's life to emphasize what could go wrong in a person's life when he's lacking composure, and what could go right for him when he's learned to compose himself. I also want to show that a lack of composure is possible for men usually known to be fairly confident, rational, and wise beyond their years. For them, it may have been a case of taking their eyes off the ball at unexpected times of their life when they were faced with a new set of circumstances that elicited previously unencountered levels of pressure.

There is, however, one thing my old and wise dad, and the radical artist, Eminem, share in common. Both men grew up in rough neighborhoods, albeit during different eras of the previous century. Today, however, things may be no different in the neighborhood Eminem grew up in. Things are no different in my dad's neighborhood, and unlike Eminem, he has stubbornly refused to move on to a more upmarket suburb, free of crime and grime.

Common Misconceptions About Composure

It's not that my dad didn't have a choice, it's just that his rational line of thinking was a case of "Why pay more?" Why expend yourself on more than you can handle? Why live in an endless cycle of debt you're never able to escape from? And why not live with a greater sense of peace of mind that others who dared to move on, sometimes wish they had? But years later, things did change in the neighborhood I grew up in. And like me, circumstances changed for my dad as well.

My dad is not someone who dwells on myths and conspiracy theories. But to be quite honest with you, I think that his habit of suppressing his emotions for most of his adult life could have been the undoing of him. As the head of the family, he might have also felt obligated to play the tough guy in tough situations, shielding what he was really thinking and feeling inside so that we didn't have to worry. But little did we know, and little did he know.

There are three misconceptions about composure I'd like you to trash before I expand on the psychological components of composure. The most common myths I'm thinking of right now are as follows:

1. Composure is only required in stressful situations.

2. Composure requires you to hold back your emotions, even in stressful situations.

3. Composure means having to strive toward perfection at all times.

Reflect on these false perceptions for a few moments and see if you can relate to them. I'm sure you can because by now, you will have had to face numerous stressful situations in your life. And as much as you've tried, it's almost impossible to be perfect. And if you've had experience at being the proverbial man of the house, you can already see that while it can be easy to keep what you're feeling about any given domestic crisis to yourself, it doesn't make you feel any better as a man.

If you come across to someone else as someone who exudes composure, he might wrongfully assume that you're mentally strong as well. In most cases, you're strong on discipline but when the going gets tough, the tough don't always get going. They crack under pressure, just like the brilliant Algerian-born soccer player Zinedine Zidane did during that epochal 2006 FIFA World Cup final against Italy.

But then again, those sportsmen who've been admirers of former bodybuilding champion, Arnold Schwarzenegger, might be inclined to disagree. That's to say that they followed his career a lot more closely than I did. Today, I acknowledge that their argument would be closer to the truth in describing the visual features of physical composure. After all, it is when the champion bodybuilder is on the stage before all to see that he must show off his confidence.

And in order for Schwarzenegger to showcase his refined muscles without raising a sweat, he would have had to utilize a lot of mental strength. It must take a great deal of mental strength to discipline yourself to do the exercises required to get you to the pinnacle, just as Schwarzenegger did. But Schwarzenegger would surely be the first to tell you that you aren't born with the mental strength to develop your physical strength. Mental strength has to be developed as well.

Psychological Components of Composure

If I'm correct in my assessment of Schwarzenegger's bodybuilding, movie, and political careers, he would also be the first to tell you that the "cowboys don't cry" analogy no longer applies. The tough guy image that many young men, including myself, grew up with, is nothing more than a facade. As a successful politician, Schwarzenegger wasn't afraid to show his emotional side. But today, I sometimes wonder what he thinks about how he managed to deceive so many admirers who bought into the tough guy image he portrayed during his rather violent and lucrative movie career.

Zinedine Zidane, on the other hand, held nothing back when he was on the football pitch. It was his sheer determination to pull out all the stops in the successful 1998 World Cup campaign that got my attention. But eight years later, I had started to wonder what was going through the aging soccer star's mind when he decided to make a comeback and help France win a second World Cup. He almost pulled it off. But then the mental screws came loose before he let the opposing player know in no uncertain terms what he thought of him crudely insulting his mother in the field of play.

Thankfully, as a successful soccer coach, Zidane has learnt to regulate his emotions. Up until the day he decided to take a break from coaching soccer, I've seen little to no evidence of him losing his self-control. If anything, all I've seen is him imposing his steely-eyed resilience across the inquisitive audience, seeking to extract further information on whether and when he intends to make a managerial comeback. Rather than leer at them, he might be inclined to share a little of his self-indulgent sense of humor. Back on the football pitch, there didn't seem to be any lack of clarity in terms of letting the players know what their goals should be, and how they should go about achieving them.

Emotional Regulation

Emotional regulation is the ability to respond to the ongoing demands of experience, using a range of emotions that are sufficiently flexible to allow spontaneous reactions. With characteristic wit, rather than head-butting the offender, Zidane, as the wise old man of football, can now retaliate with verbal cues, and without causing any offense. As a retired politician, Arnold Schwarzenegger is able to utilize emotional empathy, rather than resort to angry verbal assaults, to make it known to us why he objects to certain forms of behavior or actions that have the potential to cause harm to others.

Emotional regulation doesn't mean that we have to meekly keep quiet. One psychologist proposed that we are allowed to express ourselves accordingly, including before we feel that emotion that would usually cause us to say something that we would later come to regret. While emotion regulation is a core component of composure, emotion dysregulation is characteristic of a number of mental disorders. I know it's an extreme analogy but it could serve as a warning of how a lack of emotional control could not only negatively impact how you function within social settings but on how it impacts your personal well-being.

The unfortunate alternative to angry outbursts, later regretted, is the bottling up of emotions. It can be equally damaging, and as surprising as this may seem, is also associated with a lack of self-esteem and confidence. There's also dissatisfaction with the relationships being engaged in. All of this contributes to unnecessary suffering and lost opportunities. So, what's to be done? There are lots that can be done, and Chapter 3 will begin the process of preparing you to make a well-rounded, approachable, and self-composed man of you.

Self-Control

In the meantime, in order to succeed in life and work, in order to treat your woman like the lady she is, and in order to keep your cool under pressure, you need to exercise self-control. But what is it really? Psychologically speaking, the following three factors help us to define self-control:

1. We are able to control our behavior, resist temptation, and achieve our goals.

2. We are able to delay gratification, as well as resist unwanted actions or impulses.

3. But our self-control is a limited resource that could be depleted.

Not only do we possess self-control, we also need to learn to develop and maintain it. We know that this is necessary because it's good for our overall health and well-being. While we can accept that self-control, also defined as discipline, determination, or willpower-is partly determined by genetics, we need to be mindful that it's a skill that we need to strengthen. I believe that with practice, you can do this.

Whether you need it for work, sport, or in your relationships with others, whether friends, family members, or a potential girlfriend, let me introduce you to three key types of self-control:

1. **Impulse control**: When you have impulse control, you have the ability to manage your urges and impulses. But if you lack this ability, you may have a tendency to act out without thinking about the consequences of your irrational behavior or speech.

2. **Emotional control**: When you have emotional control, you have the ability to regulate your emotional responses. But if you struggle in this area, you may have a tendency to overreact during tense situations, allow foul moods to fester, and sometimes boil over.

3. **Movement control**: When you have movement control, you have the ability to control how and when your body needs to move. If you have difficulty in this area, you may feel restless, always finding it challenging to remain still.

As a fitness enthusiast, perhaps you can relate to the above description. There's no doubt in your mind that you want to complete a set of reps but in your over-enthusiastic determination to do more with what you've got in terms of both physical and mental strength, you end the session prematurely. On the surface, it may have looked as if Arnold Schwarzenegger and kung-fu legend, Bruce Lee, had superhuman levels of discipline and self-control but believe me, this is something that took them years to develop and master.

Like you, they wanted self-control in their lives but were prepared to work toward developing it. They knew that a lack of ability and strength could have led to a lack of willpower and were prepared to learn how to achieve it and keep it. Just think of what you could achieve with greater self-discipline. You'll do well in the gym. You'll do well on the track, and if you're still in high school, you'll be able to achieve higher grades and higher test scores, allowing you to pave the way toward a successful entry to college.

To give you a practical example of what's required, self-control means having to strive for results that allow you to exercise regularly, eat a balanced, healthy diet, become more productive, and give up all the bad habits that may have kept you back from achieving your best.

Impulse Management

Perhaps I'm luckier than others to not have such a strong interest in social media activities. It has given me the space to do more of what I want to achieve from day to day. I'm not being insensitive in remarking that others haven't been so lucky, and am not the first to tell you that excess time spent on social media is a challenging habit to break. And there are worse habits I can think of that are even more difficult to break. For instance, those who are lacking in impulse control find it harder to give up gambling, sex, drinking, or drugs. Just think, however, of what could be achieved with greater impulse management.

Thanks to my 20-minute-a-day psychology reading sessions, I slowly but surely learned how to practice impulse management. Here's how I did it. In the beginning, I worked hard to avoid situations that could trigger impulsive behavior. I learned to swallow my pride and ask for help in areas of my life where I felt I lost control. Alternative but healthier outlets were created to cater toward the impulsive side of my human nature.

But if I was already into boxing, and spent a great deal of time in the gym, how much healthier could I get? My physical health might have been acceptable to those of average strength but it was my mental strength that needed development. Hence the 20-minute-a-day reading habit I developed. That habit grew on me, and before I knew it, I was cutting back on the time I'd usually reserve for watching TV. Simply put, I wanted to read more. I wanted to learn more. I wanted to do more with the time that I had.

As I said earlier, perhaps I've been luckier than others. But for others, behavioral and talk therapy can be an invaluable tool to help them get their impulses under control. For impulse management to be successful within a controlled and safe counseling environment, both the therapist and his client will need to take into account the client's current mental health, his surrounding environment and circumstances, and even genetics. If these exist, substance use issues would have to be addressed as a matter of priority.

Inhibitory Control

Previously, inhibitory control was primarily focused on people who were diagnosed with attention deficit hyperactivity disorder (ADHD), but there's no reason why you can't utilize it to help you take control of your life with levels of composure not experienced before. To alleviate any misunderstanding about this function, note that inhibitory control is not related to sexual inhibition but can be utilized to control natural urges that could disrupt you from functioning normally.

Psychologically speaking, inhibitory control is described as a core executive function that helps you to control automatic urges. These are related to your behavior, your thoughts and emotions, and your ability to pay attention to what you're doing. You can also use inhibitory control to think about past experiences to help you consider the consequences of a future action or set of circumstances.

Interestingly, you're already developing inhibitory control within the first year of your life. It develops quickly until you've reached the age of six and will continue developing for the next 20-30 years of your life. Also, you can use cognitive inhibitory control to control your focus and attention. Behavioral inhibitory control, on the other hand, is your ability to control your urges, and react and respond to situations when you know it wouldn't be appropriate for you to do so. Motor inhibitory control is your ability to control your motor behavior. It's a form of discipline that keeps you rooted in the task designated to you, while emotional inhibitory control is used to control or regulate your emotions.

Finally, if you have low cognitive inhibitory control, you're easily distracted and find it difficult to pay attention. Low behavioral inhibition leads to impulsivity, while low motor inhibition could be a form of hyperactivity.

Self-Monitoring

At this stage, don't worry too much if you find it difficult to pay attention or control your impulses. In future chapters, I'll show you how you can gain the upper hand in such cases. In the meantime, let me introduce you to the use of the journal. Journaling your thoughts, tasks, and actions on a daily basis is a great way to help you gain control of your life. Using a journal, you'll be regularly monitoring your thoughts and actions. Regular note-taking is also a form of cognitive behavior. While writing down what you see and think about, you're attempting to gain clarity about what you're doing, why you're doing the task in front of you, what you've done in the past, and how the completion or not of your task has affected you.

Whether you use a journal, diary or choose to compose your thoughts during a walk or on the gym floor, the self-monitoring process is a natural part of your personality. But self-monitoring is also subject to abuse in the sense that you could be prone to excessive self-criticism. Letting yourself down over past failures is hardly helpful but correct self-monitoring can help you in leaps and bounds. But if you're able to adjust well to the concept of self-monitoring, as introduced by psychologist Mark Snyder during the 1970s, you'll be able to positively influence your behavior in different situations. The following are typical of someone who is self-assuredly monitoring himself:

- You'll be able to gain attention or approval from others through your speech.

- You're also prepared to change your opinions, provided that it doesn't negate your values or beliefs, in order to gain the favor of others.

- If necessary or appropriate to do so, you can imitate the behavior of others.

- You'll monitor the behavior of others to identify a correct course of action.

- You're prepared to seek advice from others in order to make correct or appropriate decisions.

- Depending on the people you're with or the situations you're in, you're prepared to adapt your behavior if and whenever necessary.

Cognitive Clarity

I mentioned in the Introduction that, unlike impulse control, cognitive clarity is not something that's handed to us at birth. But it is a concept that can be developed. In the context of what we're trying to achieve in this book, it's necessary to help you gain confidence, control, and of course, composure. If you have cognitive clarity, your mind is clear. You're fully active and engaged, and have it within you to resolve problems, and keep yourself productive throughout the day.

But due to the pressures of daily life, we're not always there. Our mental fitness will suffer as a result. We lose sleep over challenges that we should have been applying our minds to. Higher levels of stress and anxiety also cause us to lose focus on our self-care requirements. Neglecting regular exercise and a healthy, balanced diet can, of course, further impair our ability to think straight, and remain calm and composed during challenging stages of our lives.

I remember South Africa's one-time world heavyweight boxing champion, Gerrie Coetzee losing all focus after he surprisingly beat Leon Spinks (who had previously beat the great Muhammad Ali) and Michael Dokes to win the WBA version of the world title. Not 10 months later, the South African had lost his title to another American, Greg Page. Having put on so much weight, it was as though the South African had hardly moved a muscle in training. I could never be sure whether the title had gone to his head or the weight of expectation was too heavy on him.

You need cognitive or mental clarity to help you make better decisions, and avoid having your judgment clouded with negative influences. Cognitive clarity also helps to be better organized. You're able to give priority to the things that need to be done before letting off steam to indulge your healthy impulses. Ultimately, cognitive clarity will help you to enjoy your life more. But if you feel as though your current lifestyle and circumstances are letting you down, you could utilize your developed mental abilities to make changes wherever and whenever necessary. To begin the process of enhancing your mental faculties, make sure that you're engaging in the following tasks:

- Not only do you need to clock in the recommended number of hours (seven to nine hours is good), you need to make use of proper sleep hygiene to ensure that you're going to enjoy quality sleep hours.

- Give yourself an introduction to a self-help version of cognitive behavioral therapy (CBT), and you'll be able to learn how to better manage your stress levels.

- Practice mindfulness to help you slow down and focus more consciously on being in the present, also paying particular attention to how your senses respond to your regular environment and actions.

- Work toward achieving a healthy work-life balance that allows you to find more enjoyment, fulfillment, and interest in challenging tasks that you would normally be tempted to give up on.

- You can also create an environment of clarity. This is your ability to clearly state your intentions and desires, whether to yourself or those around you. Focus on writing down your priorities and set realistic objectives to help you clear your desk of all tasks, beginning with the most mundane and easily accomplished, and finishing with the most challenging.

Under Pressure

Trying to do too much with the little you've got is going to place you under pressure. Be wary of trying to do too much and accept that you're not in a position to please everyone at the same time. To others, it might seem selfish of you but I say to you that you need to put yourself before others in the interest of your improved health and wellbeing. Remember always that if you're well, then others can be well too, particularly those who have no choice but to depend on you.

The gym where I work out and coach others is crowded at the best of times. Sometimes, just five young men will show up for training. But on others, and usually toward the end of the month, it's easy to imagine me being overwhelmed by the attention of over 20 aspiring boxers. But these days, it doesn't bother me much, and I usually give priority to those who regularly attend their training sessions at their scheduled times. All others need to get in line and wait their turn to be mentored. And if my assigned two hours have expired, then it's on them.

Before reading psychology, I learned a lot from my dad about keeping myself calm when under pressure. Today, I'm able to replicate his fine example of rationality and wisdom. That's usually at the best of times. But at the worst of times, things can go horribly wrong, even with the best preparation. I remember a time when I had to guide my dad to find a suitable parking spot when we went to visit my mother at a private clinic a few years ago. Her illness was unexpected, and my dad wasn't used to being alone at home, tending to the everyday household chores.

His mind was always someplace else, usually at my mother's bedside, so it wasn't always easy for him to pay attention to basic tasks like parking the car perfectly or ticking off the grocery shopping list. But even at an advanced age, not able to move as quickly as he used to when working, he was able to adapt. Unexpected crises notwithstanding, to my mind, aging can also impair our ability to think, behave, and act cognitively. This section seeks to emphasize what could go wrong from a mental health perspective when stress and anxiety threaten to spiral out of control.

Stress

The World Health Organization (WHO) defines stress as a state of mental tension usually caused by challenging situations. But it's also a natural response which prompts us to address the challenges and threats we're faced with. If you're feeling stressed now, don't worry. It's normal, and we all experience stress in different ways. It's also alright to respond differently to undue levels of stress at different moments. Bear in mind that stress also affects the body. If the mind's not well, its ability to control what the body does can be impaired.

While some stress is healthy for you, it can still make it difficult for you to relax. When you're not relaxed, you're prone to being irritable, sometimes even anxious. It's difficult to concentrate and focus when you're under pressure, and if stress levels are not checked, you could experience headaches or other bodily pains. If not, you may lose your appetite or find it difficult to sleep at night. I, on the other hand, am usually exhausted by the time I turn in, but sometimes find myself waking up too early. Also, there's nothing wrong with my appetite, but when stressed, I have a tendency to overeat sometimes.

Whether journaling or utilizing other forms of cognitive self-help therapy, always monitor your stress levels. Not doing so when times are particularly challenging, could lead to chronic stress. Lacking control of your thoughts and actions, you could develop an anxiety disorder and even depression. But note too that there's a distinct difference between stress and anxiety. The American Psychological Association (APA) states that while people under stress experience mental and physical symptoms, people who experience anxiety worry excessively, even when there's no physical or mental stress present.

Anxiety

While higher-than-average levels of anxiety can be managed through self-help therapy, it remains more acute than stress. So, if you're feeling anxious for prolonged periods of time, and if it feels as though your anxiety levels are spiraling out of control, and you're unable to manage it, seek help at the earliest opportunity. I realized this much about my life during my early readings on psychology. Not only conscious of my own behavior, I wanted to help some of the young men down at the gym who were having difficulty focusing on their training exercises.

I realized the irony in this struggle I was witnessing. So much for doing healthy things to take your mind off unhealthy preoccupations. That may be true but if you choose to ignore the triggers or causes of your anxiety, even when engaging in healthy activities, you're only repressing that which must be attended to before it gets any worse. Problems don't go away. They get worse if you choose to ignore them. They need to be resolved. But knowing this much about this imperative, don't let it put pressure on you. In the meantime, the APA lists the following anxiety disorders that we need to be aware of:

- **Generalized anxiety disorder**: This disorder is characterized by persistent worry or anxiety about a variety of concerns, as well as a general sense that something bad could happen.

- **Panic disorder**: This disorder is characterized by recurrent panic attacks which include physical symptoms such as sweating or shortness of breath. Such attacks usually happen without warning.

- **Phobias**: This disorder is characterized by an intense fear of objects or situations, such as snakes and spiders, or a crowded elevator in a 50-story high building.

- **Social anxiety disorder**: People with this disorder don't like being in a crowd. In social situations, they are fearful of feeling embarrassed or judged. They also feel helpless and have difficulty making new friends.

- **Obsessive-compulsive disorder (OCD)**: People with OCD are plagued by uncontrollable feelings, thoughts, routines, or rituals, with compulsive hand washing being a common example.

- **Post-traumatic stress disorder (PTSD)**: People with PTSD often lack composure after suffering severe physical or emotional trauma. A concussion suffered after a heavy blow to the head in the boxing ring is an example of physical trauma, while my mom's illness may have caused my dad excessive emotional trauma.

The Role of Composure

I can only imagine what Eminem must have felt like when he froze during his first rap battle. He lost his composure during what was described as a rap battle during one of his earliest appearances before a large crowd. But I don't believe the famous rapper was suffering from a social anxiety disorder. Rather, there appears to be evidence of PTSD due to his experiences of growing up in a particularly rough neighborhood at a younger age. Freezing on the spot in front of a large audience could also be an example of a sudden panic attack.

The same goes for freezing in the middle of the ring, no matter how much you're sweating. Excessive sweating is exacerbated by low levels of fitness, not conducive to putting up a good fight in the ring. I maintain that whether you're an amateur or aspiring professional, you must be literally 100% mentally and physically fit before competing. Concentration levels need to be at a peak, and any lack of composure, with or without protective headgear, could be dangerous. It's dangerous on the road when driving, and it's even dangerous on the proverbial soapbox when addressing a large crowd, craning their ears to hear every word you're saying. If not in a stadium, you could be in the boardroom. Saying the wrong thing in the heat of the moment could lead to others misjudging or misinterpreting you, and consequently making an incorrect decision.

If it wasn't PTSD that caused Eminem to break down, it could be because of drugs and alcohol. An excessive dependence on these substances could lead to a full-blown addiction, and the time spent between ending the last fix and acquiring the next fix could be loaded with anxiety. But I'm not going to speculate about Eminem's past. Rather, I invite you to use him as a good role model of what can go right for you when you face up to your fears, and learn to overcome them. To my mind, Eminem is a classic example of what can be achieved, and today of course, he's a strong advocate for helping young men with addiction and other mental health disorders.

Composure in Different Areas of Your Life

As this chapter draws to a close, my focus is on presenting you with as many benefits as possible. These benefits accrue when you're able to maintain composure in different areas of your life. At this stage, it's not for me to say where and when exactly you need composure because this is something you can reflect on while journaling. If you're not up to the writing task (which only requires a few minutes of your time every day), get out into the open and enjoy the fresh air. Clear your mind with fresh thoughts while walking. For some, being mobile helps to clear the mind. I do some of my best work while completing a routine walk.

Great Composure Benefits

My focus is on improved mental health. But in the following list, I've aligned areas of life where the highlighted benefit can be linked, just to give you an impression of what's usually expected of you:

- decisiveness (workplace, golfing green)

- resilience (military training, weight training)

- positivity (workplace leadership)

- confidence (speech-making)

- self-control (boxing ring, law enforcement work)

- healthier relationships (girlfriend, family)

- conflict resolution (workplace and family leadership)

- restraint (bullying)

- wealth management (business, investment)

The list of benefits is ongoing. Before turning to Chapter 2, invest some time of your own in compiling a list of benefits that resonate with your own life, addressing your personal circumstances, life goals, and relationships with others.

One of the greatest setbacks that lead to a lack of composure in men of any age, is a sudden change of life. As has happened with my dad, it happens to the best of us. It happened to me as well. A sudden change of life is regarded as a setback when everything else fails. You've put your full weight into planning for your future, and you've exercised discipline in most areas of your life, from always balancing the budget to showing up on time. Until one day, it all goes belly-up. Things not foreseen or expected happen to you.

But sometimes in life, things happen for a reason. The reason's not bad. It's good. After all, who would have thought that instead of becoming a professional boxer, I could become a successful life coach, to say nothing of coaching young men down at the gym every other evening of the week?

We need to appreciate the harsh realities of what a lack of composure can do to a person, but at the same time, we can learn to address such a shortcoming. This much was made clear to you in this chapter. The next chapter focuses on the personal challenges related to a lack of composure. But as will be the case for the rest of the book, the next chapter will also tell you what you can do to bounce back and apply composure to all areas of your life.

2. The Harsh Reality

When my dad used to give me lectures on the harsh realities of life, I sometimes tried to switch myself off from what he was trying to say. This was before I started reading psychology. My dad was still working at the time, and I think it's fair to say that he was doing quite well for himself compared to other men his age. They had all grown up in a difficult neighborhood. Compared to others, my dad's survival instincts were razor-sharp. He was disciplined. He paid the bills on time and never over-extended himself on credit. He was a rare breed of man. When the credit card was due, he'd pay the entire amount that was due. He never maxed out, and vainly, he tried to teach me that financial discipline was a core principle to survive in this world.

When I look back at my dad's life, I sometimes wonder to myself: How would he have survived during, say, the Stone Age? No money. No proper roof over our heads, other than the rudimentary structures he put together with his bare hands. No grocery stores for my mom to waste her time while my dad patiently looked for a secure parking spot outside the mall where they would usually shop in today's era. Come to think of it, no automobiles either, not even a horse and cart. No pistols or hunting rifles to hunt with and guard the homestead at night against carnivorous scavengers, as well as neighbors who couldn't have bothered to be as resourceful as I imagined my dad would be during the Stone Age.

On those days that I did, why did I try to switch myself off from the lessons of survival my dad was trying to teach me at the time? For one thing, I always believed that the message he was sending me was inherently negative. To others, he might have been doing very well for himself, but as far as I was concerned, he could have done so much more with his life. A man with his level of intelligence, diligence, and discipline would surely have been able to achieve so much more.

Of course, I was naive and as a teenager, completely ignorant of what it took to survive in a 20th-century world. All I wanted to do was mess around and box. But other than training hard at the gym every afternoon after school, what was I prepared to do to make a good boxing career possible for myself? Where was the money for my gloves, boots, and trunks going to come from? Where was the protein-rich diet that I needed to build and sustain muscle strength going to come from? And did I even have the right temperament to succeed in a competitive sport where dozens of other fighters were vying for a place on the top of the tournament bill?

When Composure Fades

After finishing high school, it didn't take me long to realize that it took a lot more than discipline and the will to succeed to be on top of the game. Part of my reluctance to accept what my dad was trying to teach me about knowing our limitations, was my naive belief that this was a form of selling ourselves short. In later years, after I started reading psychology, I stumbled across Carol Dweck's theory on the fixed mindset. As Dweck describes it, the fixed mindset is a prescribed way in which we think about our intelligence and abilities. Our intelligence levels and levels of talent are cast in stone and cannot be changed.

We are who we are and must learn to deal with it.

But alongside Dweck's fixed mindset is the growth mindset which doesn't accept failure. It doesn't accept that we must resign ourselves to not being the best. It doesn't accept that we must learn to live and survive within the mental fortress that we build around us. Our potential may be unknowable at an early stage of our growth and development but it is nevertheless, something we can strive to achieve. Short of never amounting to anything in life, the fixed mindset contributes to increased stress levels, and the pressure to perform up to other people's expectations. Anything less than that can be regarded as failure.

As I read further into Dr Dweck's concepts on the fixed and growth mindsets, I came to the conclusion that the fixed mindset becomes a stumbling block toward allowing us to conduct ourselves with composure, particularly under challenging circumstances. It also negates our ability to deal with lifestyle changes, if and when they arise, and could have a profound effect on how we look after ourselves, both at home and in the workplace. No more, no less, the fixed mindset places us in a dangerous pressure cooker of becoming ill-disciplined, and not looking after ourselves.

My dad's words of wisdom did eventually sink in. So too, my mom's assertive instructions on self-care, something many single men, if they're honest with themselves, will be ready to acknowledge are sorely lacking, and could contribute immeasurably to their success in life, if practiced just as their mothers instructed them to. Subjectively speaking, I could have pointed a finger of blame at the so-called cavemen whose only purpose was to survive. Couldn't they move out of the cave? Couldn't they pack up what little belongings they had, and search for greener and safer pastures? Of course, they could, and as they say in literature, the rest is history.

Mankind has come a long way since those prehistoric days, but sadly, they have not taken full advantage of the knowledge, skills, and resources at their disposal. This section reveals the harsh reality of our circumstances today and identifies what went wrong in at least the last 50 years of our history as human beings.

Lifestyle Changes

During their earliest days, men had no alternative but to adapt. Or die. It was as simple as that. Their fight for survival could just as easily be compared with my attempt to keep myself in the center of the ring with my feet firmly rooted on the canvas. If I allowed myself to waver, I would be backed into a corner and have no alternative but to defend myself against a barrage of predatory punches. Come to think of it, brilliant soccer coaches like Zinedine Zidane, Pep Guardiola, and Sir Alex Ferguson, speak with one voice when they say that sometimes, attack is the best form of defense.

Today, however, it's a completely different story. Today's men have a variety of takeaway, pre-tuned resources at their disposal. They also take it for granted that when things break down, there will always be someone around to fix them.

They are only a mobile call away, so there's no need to worry. They also have the financial resources to back them up. But when the money runs dry, and the credit lines are cut, what happens then? What happens if, almost overnight, they lose their jobs?

Gone are the days when we could simply pick up the broken pieces and walk into another job. It's not as simple as it was for men from my dad's generation. No amount of artificial intelligence is required to help you realize this harsh reality. Or do you still need more convincing?

We have survival instincts to fall back on. Just as it was during prehistoric times, these instincts are natural. When faced with danger, natural stress kicks in, and we're able to fight for our lives, if it comes to that. Whether we choose to use our naturally-driven stress resources or sit on our hands and let the worst happen to us we need to be aware that there are three basic human survival instincts that keep us alert and alive, namely fear, want, and a desire to jealously protect what we believe is ours.

Today, it doesn't seem fair that those with limited or no resources to speak of, have to struggle to survive in ways that our ancestors did. Unlike our ancestors, they're no longer able to rely on natural resources to put food on the table, and consequently, they're malnourished. One would have thought that we could learn a lesson from what others less fortunate than ourselves have to go through. One would have hoped that urbanized young men who admire today's African soccer stars who are doing rather nicely for themselves, could have learned what it took African migrants to get where they are today.

But no. The lesson has yet to be learned.

Dietary Challenges

Even on a shoestring budget, there's simply no excuse for us not taking better care of our dietary requirements. Today, the majority of men who never exercised a day in their lives, are overweight. Even those of us who do bother to go to the gym every other evening after work, are at risk of contracting type 2 diabetes. With more than enough food at our disposal, how is this even possible? Could it be because too many of us couldn't be bothered to cook a healthy, balanced meal when we get home at night? Rather than enjoy a home cooked meal that doesn't need to take more than 20 minutes to rustle up, could it be that too many of us prefer to order in?

And what does an ordered-in or takeout meal constitute? Plenty of greasy fat, tons of carbs that have nowhere else to go but to our waistlines, and hundreds of calories, worthy of a heart attack or stroke from which many of us have little chance of surviving. The picture painted by the US-based Centers for Disease Control and Prevention (CDC) is no less bleak. According to the CDC, nine out of ten Americans consume too much sodium. That's thanks to a diet rich in pizzas, fries, and canned food as well. Never mind young men not yet 20, but toddlers as old as two years are battling with obesity. Speaking of which, almost half the US population is obese, thanks to poor nutritional habits which also contribute to high blood pressure and high cholesterol levels.

High levels of sodium, fat, and carbohydrates are also affecting our ability to think constructively and responsibly for ourselves. Men stress more when they eat more than their share of processed red meat. Not only that, the weekend barbecue has been tarnished because more and more men are choosing to consume processed meats instead. It's enough to cause any parent with reasonable levels of responsibility and intelligence to have a heart attack.

Figuratively speaking of course, because my point is made: more and more men are placing unnecessary pressure on themselves by allowing their stress and anxiety levels to spiral out of control, to say nothing of those who prematurely succumb to depression. No matter how stressful our lives are (and remember always that there's such a thing as healthy stress), we add more misery to our lives by giving in to our junk food cravings. Research has shown that the type of food we consume will have a profound effect on our moods, and it's common knowledge that a healthy, balanced diet, like the Mediterranean diet, promotes better mental health, as opposed to unhealthy eating habits which contribute to the deterioration thereof.

The harsh reality of all of the above must surely have given you food for thought. But as to our gradual mental deterioration, as well as the decline of our physical health, there's still more to add to this unfortunate episode of modern 21st-century life.

Technology and the Surrounding Environment

Long before I read about the philosophy, my old dad had already explained that as reluctant as he is to embrace 21st-century technologies like online banking apps and autonomous-driving SUVs, the tools that we have at our disposal are only as good as their users. As far as I'm concerned, instead of enhancing our ability to think out of the box and do smarter things, today's technologies, and the surrounding sociological environment that makes it possible, have also contributed to our mental decline.

One evening after training, I was asked to give a quick talk about addiction. I had no time in which to prepare my talk but was able to quickly compose myself, thanks to a background knowledge of what the young men wanted to talk about. Apart from junk food cravings, they had grave concerns about drug and alcohol addiction. Coming from a similar background, I could relate to what was on their minds. But at the top of my mind was an addiction to the online environment.

Instead of doing proper rest and recuperation exercises in between bouts and reps on the weights floor, some of the chaps were on their mobiles. This used to irritate me a lot. But rarely did I show my displeasure in a way that would make

Muhammad Ali's legendary trainer, Angelo Dundee, shudder with delight. After all, just like Ali, I had learned to compose myself. Nevertheless, there they were, on their mobiles, seemingly engrossed in their favorite social media feeds which had absolutely nothing to do with boxing.

Pornography and online gambling is another concern of mine. For many men, pornography has substituted their inability to find themselves a steady girlfriend to lean on in good and bad times. Gambling started out as nothing more than a desperate drive to make some money to compensate for not having steady jobs to wake up to in the morning.

Whether or not you've finished high school, there's simply no excuse to not take up one or two literary interests, as opposed to relying too much on fake news. Just think what no more than 20 minutes of daily reading could do for your ability to distinguish not only between fact and fiction but between what's right and what's wrong. Whether cooking for yourself, meeting someone in person, or making a door-to-door effort to find steady work, isn't it better to rely on the human touch? After all, I doubt very much whether a bot is going to be able to train you like Dundee did Ali back in the day.

What Happened to Our Testosterone Levels and Why

Poor dietary habits and a lack of exercise and proper sleep have also contributed toward a universal drop in men's testosterone levels. Too much reliance on modern appliances and modes of transportation has also contributed to a drop in what is essentially a key ingredient required to be able to work, play, and live as a healthy, balanced, well-rounded man should. After all, we require sufficient levels of testosterone in our bodies to regulate sperm production, and build and maintain strong muscles.

Apart from all the health and wellness concerns that surround us these days, there's another concern I have about the yearly drop in testosterone levels among men. Many men who think they have enough testosterone to defeat a horde of barbarians don't believe in what we've come to term as global warming and climate change. Contrary to what they think, there's more than enough evidence to show that human behavior is the root cause of rising temperatures and pollution levels.

Thanks to our dependence on modern technological conveniences, we've become tardy. We might remember to take out the trash before the garbage disposal truck arrives, but do we remember to recycle? Thanks to a growing food fad that shouts out convenience, more and more of our groceries are consumed by plastic wrapping. Plastic bottles, food storage containers, detergents, and even the liners of metal food containers, contain a harmful set of ingredients known as endocrine-disrupting chemicals (EDCs). As their name suggests, they're chemicals that interfere with the human body's hormones.

Not only do these harmful substances affect our ability to produce healthy semen and testosterone levels, they also affect our immunity and metabolism.

But here's a contributing factor that almost blew me away, figuratively speaking of course. Thanks to the Surgeon General's ongoing health warnings, and legislation that forbids the commercial promotion of these products, as well as banning people from smoking them in public places, the consumption of tobacco continues its steady decline. You would, of course, agree that this is good news. But what does it have to do with declining testosterone levels in men?

What Happens When Composure Is Lost

I've already told you that my dad was renowned for his visible manifestation of composure. When he was around, we all knew that we were safe. At least, that's how I felt when I was still too young to tie my own shoelaces, let alone lace up a pair of boxing gloves. But let me not dwell on Dad's story. Let me continue with one of the famous stories from the annals of sporting history. Cast your mind back to the 2006 FIFA World Cup Final one balmy evening in Germany.

Because of their pedigree, France was the favorite to win the World Cup a second time. But in all honesty, most soccer fans believed that the gilt-edged French had one special ingredient that the cagey, defense-minded Italians lacked: Zinedine Zidane. The pundits were also proved correct in their analogy of one of the classiest players to have ever graced the football field. But we've spoken enough about Zidane. In terms of losing your composure when it counts the most, nothing could be more cynical than the sending off of not one but three great players in three separate encounters.

Not for nothing was fellow Frenchman, Eric Cantona, nicknamed Kung Fu Cantona. Unlike Zidane whose temper quite literally got to his head, Cantona took out his frustration on a loud-mouthed fan, sitting on the sidelines of the pitch. It was a sight for sore eyes, to say the least. Not only did Cantona disgrace himself in front of millions of forgiving fans around the globe, he got himself banned from playing for at least a full season.

Returning to the World Cup stage, English talisman, Wayne Rooney appeared to have lost it as well after a particularly nasty foul on his Portuguese nemesis, Cristiano Ronaldo, a player who needs little to no introduction to today's young football fans. But it wasn't Rooney's foul that caught my attention. Rather, it was the unsportsmanlike behavior of Ronaldo who appeared to stage a dive that deceived the under-pressure referee to flash the red card.

To my mind, blatant cheating, not necessarily premeditated, is a sign of a sportsman losing his composure. But there can be nothing worse than bloody violence as a sign of someone completely losing it. Not for the first time did Uruguayan striker, Luis Suarez, cause more than a stir when he proceeded to chew yet another player in the 2014 FIFA World Cup, hosted by Brazil. In two previous incidents at league football level, Suarez was in the thick of goal-mouth player-biting incidents. On the sporting field, these incidents must surely rank as one of the worst examples of a player losing his composure.

Sadly, there have been far more serious incidents away from the playground. For instance, Columbian soccer star, Andres Escobar, was gunned down and killed by a raving mad fan after the defeated Columbians returned home from the US-hosted 1994 World Cup. Perhaps Escobar had momentarily lost his composure when he scored an own goal that cost the national team dearly.

Common Stressors

There's a lesson to be learned from Suarez's violent and unsportsmanlike conduct. As far as records go, he received no less than three banning's since the first biting incident. One would have thought that after the first incident, the lesson Suarez should have learned, was learned. It couldn't have been. After all, he went on to repeat his outrageous behavior. Could it have been that the banning's were too soft? Should football's governing bodies have issued a lifetime ban instead? After all, others have been banned for life for offenses warranted to be serious enough for such harsh penalties, so why not him?

The only lesson I could take from the leniency shown toward the Uruguayan is that if there were interventions to correct his behavior, they were ineffective. Also, while he is still playing the game, he remains a poor role model for all the young admirers who effectively have chosen to turn a blind eye to his behavior. To my mind, Suarez's lack of composure, as well as decorum, is indicative of both internal and external stressors. While there's no evidence that Suarez thought about committing such actions before carrying them out, his unsportsmanlike behavior on the pitch (there have been other incidents) does show that he was insecure. Finally, there's no doubt that the much-admired player was under pressure to perform on the highest stage.

But then again, no matter what sport they play, whether Lebron James on the basketball court or Tyson Fury in the ring, most of today's superstars are under pressure to perform. While results are expected, surely it's also an expectation that they compose themselves well in a manner that can be replicated by young admirers.

The above "sporting" stories surely provide enough evidence of what happens to a man when all composure is lost due to the manifestation of both internal and external stressors. But what are internal stressors? And what are external stressors? Let's take a look at these from a psychological perspective. On the surface, internal stressors come from the way men think in the heat of the moment, while external stressors refer to the pressure they feel in the workplace or during their relationships with others.

Internal stressors are sources of stress that reside within us. These are the thoughts and feelings that quickly come to mind when you're feeling uneasy about a situation or set of circumstances. Uncertain about what to do in such stressful situations, you too could be feeling insecure. Lacking the coping skills required to extricate yourself from harsh situations, you could sink into a sense of low self-esteem, and if you're thinking about what to do to help get you out of the jam you're in, you're usually thinking too much in a way that is wholly irrational and unproductive, yielding no positive results.

External stressors, on the other hand, are sources of stress that surround you. While you're aware of the pain they could be causing you, you're anxious and lack any sense of direction on how to deal with traumas when they occur, and even everyday hassles that other men with composure would have little difficulty in resolving.

Common Displays and Results

Looking at stress from a slightly different perspective, I can think of no less than four different types of stress which you could also relate to if you're able to set aside time to assess how you've been performing lately in your daily life. While I provide my own examples, you can look at the following types of stress, and pick out areas of your life where you've been finding it difficult to cope:

- **Physical Stress**: This type of stress can also occur when you've overextended yourself in the gym. Trying to lift more than your fair share of weights, you push yourself to the limit and risk injury. But when you're stressed internally, your increased pulse rate may have little to do with any physical weight you're carrying.

- **Mental Stress**: Surrounded by too much noise in a crowded mall, it can be difficult to concentrate when you're in the middle of a meeting. Cramming for an exam the night before is hardly ideal preparation, and the pressure this causes, causes the tardy student to forget memorized answers in the exam. Speaking of which, rote learning at any stage of higher learning, is hardly ideal either.

- **Emotional Stress**: Whether in the boxing ring or in the middle of a heated argument not caused by you, the "fight or flight" response may have been healthy if you knew how to react. But lacking composure, you may be fearful, angry, or frustrated instead.

- **Behavioral stress**: Whether you're engaged in healthy pursuits like circuit training in the gym or going on a bike ride, or indulging in unhealthy habits like overeating junk food over the weekend, you're placing stress on your body. Unhealthy habits like smoking or drinking late at night are unwholesome but impractical responses to the usual or extreme pressures of life.

Of course, you're allowed to relax over the weekend to recover from another challenging week at the office but if the things you're doing over the weekend are harmful to your physical and mental health, you could find yourself under even more pressure by the following Monday morning, particularly if you've been having too many late nights, and haven't been able to get a decent night's sleep for as long as you can remember. Or perhaps you can't remember at all? Memory loss is an acute sign that you're over-stressed.

Poor Composure

Apart from lashing out angrily at someone for no other reason than your innate frustration at your own inability to gain control over high-pressure situations or circumstances, there are still more signs to look out for to show that you're lacking composure. Apart from an inability to concentrate and remember things, particularly when under pressure, the following physical gestures and emotional reactions, show that your composure remains poor and needs to be addressed:

- Whether in a meeting or a heated argument, you find it difficult to maintain eye contact. If you're not speaking too quickly, stumbling over your words, your speech is slurred. You also find it difficult to listen to what others are saying. If not that, you don't want to know what they're saying.

- Agitated or anxious, your breathing is shallow or rapid. Others can also see that you're tense and find it difficult to relax, even under normal circumstances.

- If you're a man of few words, no matter what the circumstances, you might have a habit of clenching your jaw. If not that, you tense your muscles as if you're about to go into a seizure.

- Perceiving that you're a failure in meetings or conflicts, you go out of your way to avoid people. Whether livid or sad, you're tired of the confrontation. But sudden changes of mood without the help of others, leave you no peace.

- Others may perceive that things are going well for you. But still, they wonder. Why are you always worrying? If you're not worrying about how to get yourself out of trouble (you might not even be in trouble; you just think that you are), you're obsessing over your version of the finer details of getting everything that you do perfectly.

- Trying to be perfect all the time, and trying to please everyone all the time, but failing, and without thinking about your health and personal wellbeing, is enough to overwhelm you. If it doesn't overwhelm you, you're usually irritated by minor inconveniences or disruptions to life as you see it.

Instead of trying to be positive to help improve your circumstances, you're prone to harshly criticizing your behavior and perceived lack of performance in many areas of your life. Lacking confidence and self-esteem, you have no difficulty in undermining yourself. On the other hand, you may be someone whose ego is inflated beyond the realms of what it means to be reasonable. This narcissistic tendency is not only a danger to you, it's a danger to others. Instead of internalizing your negative self-talk, you're prone to harshly criticizing others. If you were a man in charge, you would have no hesitation in firing the person who has allegedly offended you.

But in such a scenario, you're clearly not in charge.

One man who clearly wasn't in charge back in the 80s was American tennis star, John McEnroe. It's worth mentioning this tempestuous player because he was involved in one of the most epic Wimbledon finals ever. He was up against five-time champion, Björn Borg. Back then, he was nick-named the "Iceborg." Cool, calm, and composed, he simply never seemed to cave into pressure. And when McEnroe came back the following year to finally defeat the Swede, it looked as though the Swede shrugged his shoulders and said to himself, "Oh well, you can't win them all."

Personality

Whether healthy or not, your daily habits could be ingrained and not acquired. That's because the habits you're prone to committing yourself to, form an integral part of who you are as a man. Your personality has everything to do with the way you behave in public, as well as behind closed doors. We have been led to believe that we are all born with a unique personality. I believe that that is essentially a good quality to have. After all, life would be really boring if we all thought and acted the same.

Some people are born leaders, while others prefer to operate in the shadows. Some of us are extroverted and have no difficulty in expressing ourselves in word and deed. But others, like you, may be introverted. The suggestion was made that an introverted nature could contribute to someone's habitual lack of composure. But at the same time, there's no doubt in my mind that an extroverted man can lack composure as well. Internally, the extroverted man is bleeding, figuratively speaking, of course, and since a young age, he's been able to mask his insecurities by imposing himself onto others.

Not for the world would I want you to change your personality. But if your personality's at fault in terms of you losing your cool or composure in the public eye, there's no reason why you can't develop it. You don't need to self-correct. All you need to do is tweak little areas of your inner self here and there. This, as well as addressing bad habits, is something we'll talk about in later chapters.

In the meantime, we still need to look at how our personalities, as well as our habit-performing behaviors, take shape. Firstly, the American Psychological Association (APA) defines personality as enduring characteristics and behavior that enable us to adjust to life, have interests, develop values, a sense of self, as well as emotional patterns. But still, where does our personality come from? And are we born with the personality we have?

Habits

For that matter, who or what influences our tendencies to form habits? Are we born with an innate sense of habit? Interestingly, while genes are inherited, personality is not. Hence, we're not born with a fixed personality. The effect of genes on daily behavior depends on the context of life, and not on you personally. So, if you're not born with an innate sense of personality, the habits you practice today are not an accurate reflection of who you are as a human being. You're not born with a prescribed set of habits either. But your habits do form when new behaviors become automatic and with little to no conscious awareness. Behavioral patterns that are repeated more often than not are, quite literally, etched into our neural pathways.

Habits are not bad, they're not something that you need to discard. Habits are necessary, but some habits are worse than others. These are the habits that are harmful to your health and well-being, and yes, they need to be discarded at the earliest opportunity. Of course, it would be humanly impossible to kiss your bad habit of skipping breakfast before a morning workout at the gym, goodbye overnight. It will require time to develop alternative behavioral patterns that allow you to get used to new, healthy habits without a great deal of discomfort.

Perhaps giving up cigarette smoking is a better example. I know from experience how difficult it was for my dad to give up smoking after smoking for most of his life. It was a habit he started during high school, and while he tried to give it up a few times, it was a habit that he couldn't break. While he never said as much, the old excuse given by so many who have tried but failed is that it's the pressure of life. It is also ironic in the sense that I've seen how relaxed and composed some of these folks become after lighting a cigarette.

But the moment only lasts for, well, a few moments, and it's not long before the cravings for another puff returns. I also think it's the sense of anxiety or agitation of not being able to smoke for long periods of time that places extra pressure on the smoker. But I'm led to understand that the habit of smoking, more so drug-taking, is a lot more complex than the seemingly innocent ritual of checking in and out into one's favorite social media account.

Even so, the ritual associated with the habit is universally applied. Researchers at the Massachusetts Institute of Technology (MIT) discovered a neurological pattern that is at the root of the ritual. It involves three steps which can be summarized as follows:

1. Cue: This is the trigger that tells the brain to go into automatic mode, prompting the behavior to unfold.

2. Routine: This is the actual behavior, and the action taken to make it happen.

3. Reward: Reward tells the brain whether a particular habit loop is worth remembering or not.

Consequences of Lacking Composure

But if you're lacking composure, isn't it easier to forget that you're due another fix? Of course not. Having immediate or latent rewards, habits are easier to pick up and condition. But delayed habits are more difficult to commit to and maintain. If you're a gym enthusiast who just happens to be a smoker as well, you might be able to relate to this. Whether you're stressed or not, your cigarettes are never far away from you, and when the craving returns, you won't hesitate to pick out another cigarette from the pack on your desk, coffee table, or side pocket, and light up again.

But knowing full well that you might need to exercise more as a result of skipping one too many weight training and circuit training sessions, you might be inclined to delay your return to the gym until the following week. You deceive yourself into believing that a weekend pass will do you good. After all, you're resting, and you're recuperating from the challenging week you've just had. But instead of proper rest, you're out with the boys, drinking and smoking, one late night after the next.

This, of course, takes its toll on what should have been a healthy mind and body. Not only are you lacking the composure required to discipline yourself into action, but you've entered a downward spiral that makes it even more difficult for you to make a comeback.

Before I conclude this chapter, let me remind you of what happens when you lose your composure. Let me remind you of what it feels like to cave into fear and pressure. Not only has your health gone for a ball of chalk, you've lost track of your goals. In the above health and fitness scenario, your goal was to improve your muscle composition and strength. But the drinking and smoking habits also negatively impacted what should have been a healthy, balanced diet, with an emphasis on both lean meat and complex carbs. Late nights being the order of the day, pizzas, burgers, and fries replaced healthy greens. The morning smoothie was forgotten, and an ice-cold can of highly sugared soda became your ineffective cure for a hangover.

Let's also assume that your motivation had little to do with hanging out with the boys. Rather, you wanted to use the late weekend nights out as an opportunity to meet girls. It's easier to meet girls at night than during the day when you're stone-cold sober. Or so you thought. All thoughts of you being shy and unattractive went out the door after you started to lose your inhibitions. Nothing, it seemed, could hold you back. But then again, most of the girls you feasted your eyes on, didn't appear to show much interest. No muscles, and a bulging waistline. More specifically, no personality and slurred words are completely misunderstood.

Let's also assume that you went further than most average guys who've never seen the inside of a gym. You did the gentlemanly thing and secured a date. You went on another date and another. Things seemed to be going quite well for you and the girl. Until one late night, you mutually decided that "tonight's the night." Except, of course, it wasn't quite right. No libido to speak of, and short of Viagra, there was just no way you were going to please her.

You never heard from her again.

You were late for work the following Monday morning. And the next Monday after that, and so on, and so forth, until you started receiving written warnings that felt more like death threats. Your beating heart told you that your world was about to end. Things were about to change. Things were going to get worse, not better. You pleaded with your boss as though your life depended on it. He wasn't having any of it. After all, completely lacking composure and any resemblance of sincerity or contrition, you had excommunicated any ability to communicate effectively and persuasively.

Out on the street, it gets a lot worse for you. Men you would usually avoid are harassing you. You don't fully understand what it is they want from you. After all, you have nothing. You lost it all. You lost it all at your last chance saloon. You gambled your life away as an ill-composed incompetent. Finally, you're left alone. Completely alone, as it turns out. You have time to think about what happened to you and why it happened. Instead of "what-if" questions, you're asking yourself "if-only" questions.

If only I had more confidence. If only I was more self-assured. If only I wasn't such a coward? If only I had a spine. And so on, and so forth. Harsh words indeed. This is the harsh reality of the downward spiral that could occur for a man who completely lacks composure and chooses to do absolutely nothing about it. This could have been you, but no, there's no need to worry because from this moment on, you're going to do something about your lack of confidence and the fear that reigns in your heart.

And from the next chapter onward, I'm going to help you do just that.

3. Strategies for Developing Composure

You have to feel for guys who lost their way. Lacking composure, they appeared to be powerless to do anything about the harsh realities of their life. Me, on the other hand, well, I had mixed feelings about such situations. It wasn't as though I was lacking empathy. It's just that I was thinking about what my dad said about being in a tough situation. His argument was that it's a tough world out there, and that, really, only I could help myself. For a while, I enjoyed my old man's tough-minded approach to life.

But then life got tougher. At the same time, I grew up. I became more aware of my surroundings. I became more aware of the hardships others go through. And one of the best lessons I learned about making it out of a tight corner in one piece, is that it's okay to ask for help.

It's my belief that a truly tough guy is capable of shedding his prideful scales. My thoughts here are also a reflection of what it takes to be a true leader. Some may well be born. But others can be developed. I'll talk about leadership in a later chapter. In the meantime, circumstances may not always allow for you to rely on the help of others, so yes, of course, my dad may be right.

After all, if you've been diagnosed with a social anxiety disorder by a public health psychotherapist who listened to your story with both their ears and their heart, you may be in no position to take advantage of the recommended private care costs. So, if you're able to develop a reasonable amount of self-confidence, I see no reason why you can't practice your own unique version of self-help.

Then again, in order to make sure that your self-help program is effective, you'll still be relying on the help of others. After all, a self-composed man can't profess to know everything there is to know about being a man. Part of being a decent man, always able to stand on his own two feet, is the willingness to always practice self-care. And yes, that does mean doing your own laundry. Doing your own washing by hand is not a task reserved for housewives, and if you ask me, it's pretty good exercise as well.

Self-care can also be used as an effective tool to help you change your identity. As for the rest of this chapter, it will of course, be an exercise in self-help because you'll be learning how to effectively regulate your emotions, control your impulses, and learn to better discipline yourself so that you can take better care of yourself. Come to think of it, self-care is also a feature of this chapter, in which case, I'll be reminding you of the health and wellness outcomes you should be striving toward in order to regain your composure, and keep it intact.

In the previous chapter, I declared that the personality you have is not cast in stone. It is subject to change. So, if you grew up being a shy, introverted little boy, you can alter your mindset to give yourself the space to transform yourself into a confident, self-assured young man.

Changing Your Identity

We all have an identity. I have mine, and you have yours, and it's what makes us different from each other. But not in a bad way, not by a long shot. Sports wise, the great Wayne Gretzky couldn't have been any different from the late, great Muhammad Ali. Come to think of it, unless I've been wearing blinkers during the time that I've watched these two great men perform, I've never seen Gretzky throw a single punch. Even if he did, I'm sure it was always about defense.

Seriously though, you couldn't have found a more self-composed hockey player than the NHL legend. But Gretzky and Ali did at least have one thing in common: mind games.

Can You Really Change Who You Are?

Using their mental game plan to the full, both Gretzky and Ali could change the course of a contest within seconds. As human beings, both men could change if they wanted to, and they did. But the question I'm asking you is: Can we really change who we are inside?

I'm sure we can. Through personal growth, with a commitment to self-reflection, and openness to feedback from others, we all have the capacity to not only change but improve our lives. Also, life-changing habits are also fortuitous in the sense that habits are already deeply ingrained within us.

Thinking and Standing on Your Own Two Feet

There's no doubt in my mind that your ability to stand on your own two feet will go a long way toward providing you with everything that you need in this life of yours. But just think how much further you could go if not only did you stand on your own two feet, you thought on your own two feet as well.

Thinking before you speak is a wise move too. But while we'll be focusing on effective communication skills in the next chapter, I sometimes wonder to myself if this wise, premeditated strategy is sincere. No, there cannot be any fault in this, and I'm adamant that a good rehearsal before the event is a good sign that you're composing yourself well.

Developing Your Formula for Identity Change

Particularly if your past behavior has been poor, there's nothing wrong with giving yourself an identity makeover as well. If you were attempting to change or end poor habits previously but failed miserably, it could be because you were motivated to change for the wrong reason. And one of the most important fundamentals in favor of positive change that succeeds is that you must want to change.

Yes, I agree: Wanting to change can sometimes be a tough ask. But if we could understand the fundamentals of change a little better, would it make a difference? I believe it could. Also, note that change occurs at three different stages, namely changing outcomes (losing weight would be a good example), changing the processes required to allow the desired change (more time spent in the gym is another good example), and the final but deepest level of change that will occur are the internal changes you undergo. These are all related to judgments about yourself, your self-image, and changing your belief system to ensure that these personal impressions of yourself are positive.

Understanding Poor Composure Traits

If the lack of composure expressed by temperamental and insecure football stars has taught us anything about poor composure, it is this: While physical composure is certainly an important component of balance and timing in sport, I believe mental composure is even more important.

Indeed, there's a reason why some guys get to be captains of their teams. They're the complete opposite of the intolerably temperamental characters I described in the previous chapter. They're cool, calm, and collected. Lebron James' shoulders may have sagged during the final quarters of so many playoff games he lost but have you noticed how the LA Lakers star would always rise to the occasion?

While you lift yourself up like James did, remind yourself that poor composure leads to the following physical and mental challenges:

- Anxiety

- Burnout

- Fatigue

- Stress

How to Remove Poor Composure Traits

You'd swear James was on the winning side. The Lakers star does, however, remind me of the great Larry Bird of Boston Celtics fame. The one common denominator that comes to mind is that practice makes perfect, and I seem to recall an anecdote about Bird being up at the crack of dawn, down at the court, shooting one hoop after the next.

I don't know about you but I'd be bored stiff repeating the same moves over and over again for at least an hour. But so it goes on the punching bag down at the gym as well. So, the lesson to you is that not only does practice make perfect but that patience becomes a virtue for you as well.

Understanding Good Composure Traits

Work hard at sharpening your mental agility as well. This is something that Wayne Gretzky, a four-time Stanley Cup winner did so well back in the day. Interestingly enough, most of the good work was done off the rink. It was Gretzky's version of locker-room talk, in which case the team captain would spend time alone developing his game plan.

Gretzky's game plan review would be indicative of one of the all-time greatest mindset tools, namely visualization. So, to switch ourselves off from the sporting metaphor for a moment, if you felt that you were lacking in composure, you could actually set aside time to visualize having composure. If you were in Gretzky's shoes, you'd be visualizing yourself executing a good pass, defending your zone, and even scoring a goal for the team but never an own goal.

How to Apply Good Composure Traits

Particularly when I'm feeling inspired, I sometimes like to call a halt to training and show the guys re-runs of what famously became known as The Thriller in Manila. This was the epic 1970s heavyweight championship duel between the powerful Joe Frazier and the aging Muhammad Ali. But even then, Ali was playing a mental game that allowed him to outwit Frazier.

While he could no longer float like a butterfly, he could still sting like a bee. The tiring, mature champ no longer needed to rely on verbal taunts to distract Frazier. All he needed to do was have faith in his abilities, honed through years of practice, and remain as calm and poised in boxing's ring of fire for as long as possible before a gap opened up for him to deliver a killer blow.

Finally, remind yourself of what it really takes to develop and apply good composure traits to your life by observing the following features thereof:

- Adaptation

- Confidence

- Cognitive excellence

- Emotional control

- Fitness

- Support

How to Effectively Regulate Your Emotions

It turns out that I'm under a bit of pressure. Once again, I've tried to do too much. My motivations may have been strong but they were also wrong. There's no denying that the book contracts I land are going to help those who read the books that I produce, but I would be lying if I denied that I was motivated to make extra cash.

It's more than I can reasonably manage. That's to say that the work that I'm doing today cannot be completed within a normal nine-to-five schedule. But I still have to manage to work around my gym hours. It's pressure alright but for me, it's healthy pressure that I can manage well these days.

Importance of Emotional Regulation in Under-Pressure Situations

Try your best to adopt the old mantra that says: Less is more. Don't feel guilty about it, and just get on with the business of regulating your emotions. Once you've done your homework, and given yourself more than enough time and practice to become a master of your own destiny, you can sit back and look at the results you've achieved with awe and wonder but never lose stock of who you are as a man.

Emotion regulation is a self-regulatory process which people use to monitor their emotions at both conscious and subconscious levels. Use it well as you develop new strategies that will help you to maintain and change necessary or required emotions at appropriate times, and particularly when you're under pressure, whether through your own doing or through circumstances beyond your control.

You can use two established motivations to help you regulate your emotions, namely hedonic and instrumental motivations. When you use your hedonic motivation, you're helping yourself to feel better. So, if you're working out on the machines in the gym, you've responded well to both your pleasure and pain receptors. You're now ready to move on to the next stage of your training. You're also looking forward to the next training goal you've set for yourself. But instrumental motivation may not be ideal for you if you're lacking motivation. Lacking motivation, the goal you set for yourself may be perceived as too challenging to deal with. Instrumental motivation is better suited for a confident man who's already motivated. He feels that he can deliver better results when working under pressure. I could relate to this but can confirm that it's no easy task having to up-regulate stress levels in order to boost performance levels.

Particularly when you've reached middle age, this steely resolve to get things done, come what may, can also take a physical toll on you. So, even when your composure levels are on the rise, remind yourself to give yourself a mental reboot by utilizing your emotional intelligence, self-awareness, self-regulation, and self-motivation in a balanced and responsible manner.

How to Identify and Understand Your Triggers

In Chapter 1, I suggested that you start using a journal to help you monitor your behavior. Now, I'd like to suggest that you use your journal to identify those moments in your life that cause you to slide. Better still, why don't we create a separate journal altogether? We'll call it our trigger journal, and I like to think that using a separate entry point for monitoring thoughts, processes, and the reasons behind them, gives us the space to compartmentalize, and declutter different areas of our lives. It's not that we're dim-witted and inherently lacking in mental clarity, it's just that the list of triggers we find may be too much to process at any given time.

But what is a trigger, I hear you ask. A trigger is anything that causes you grief. It's usually a mental stimulus that causes a painful or unpleasant memory to resurface. It's also a sensory reminder (the sound of a barking dog or a gun going off) that something's about to happen. And when it happens, it could be dangerous. Finally, it's important that you take a level-headed approach toward triggers. That said, you can also use your journal to remind yourself that you're safe, and no harm will be done to your developing self-composure, just as long as you accept yourself for who you are, and also accept the circumstances you're faced with. Finally, be kind to yourself, and don't let anything or anyone get to you.

How to Express Your Emotions Appropriately

Let's be honest. When we're under pressure, we don't always express ourselves appropriately, and tragically, it sometimes happens that whenever we lash out angrily, our anger is directed toward someone we love. We, of course, end up hurting that person the most. For me personally, it's almost cowardly in the sense that instead of composing myself in a "cool, calm, and collected" manner, using all the self-help tools at my disposal, to direct my objections at the perceived guilty offender, I'm causing harm, however unintended, to an innocent bystander.

Practicing Mindfulness: The Things You Can Do

Mindfulness interventions will be a great way to redirect your anger and frustration in the right direction. One of my brothers who has anger management issues of his own, once said to me that he takes his frustrations out on an online war game. I had to wonder out aloud whether this was healthy, and did suggest that he try the punching bag down at our gym instead.

Even so, there are more salient and peaceful ways to let off steam or recompose yourself. You don't necessarily have to follow the mindfulness practice conventions to the letter, you might not have the time and patience to meditate; it can take a while to master this art, just as long as you're doing something that you enjoy. It will, of course, be something within reason, and should stimulate the mind. I speak from experience when I say that mental stimulation equals mental calm.

How to Achieve Cognitive Clarity

Most of the guys I coach down at the gym are young enough to be my own sons. Because my time at the gym is limited—two hours of coaching the guys, and then if I'm lucky, another hour or two all to myself—there's little time for social interactions with men my own age. There are, however, those rare pearls when the gym's grown quiet, usually over weekends or at times of the month when most of the gym's attendees are running helter-skelter around town, trying to eke out a living.

I would say that there are not more than half a dozen men my age in regular attendance at our gym, usually preoccupied with the weights and circuit machines. Half of them always appear to be going through the motions but that's their affair. As long as they're happy and they're not over-extending themselves on the weights. And then there are those who appear to know what they're doing. They're not self-conscious about their physical appearance, nor are they seeking to break any records. All they're doing is keeping themselves trim and fit. And happy.

Men in positions of responsibility with the weight of the world on their shoulders. And yet still, their calm demeanor gives me the impression that while they treat their responsibilities with the seriousness it requires, they're taking these responsibilities in their stride. Their sessions are always well-timed out of due consideration for others who also need to use the gym equipment. These sessions last no longer than 45 minutes to an hour at the most.

As limited as their time appears to be, they always have time for the odd locker-room joke or two but are mindful of crossing the red line in terms of using crude language that is disrespectful of those who are different from them, particularly those who are less fortunate than they are. They're respectful of women, particularly the few well-muscled girls who, visiting our gym as fully paid-up members, have sporting aspirations of their own.

One quiet late Saturday afternoon, as I was cleaning some of the equipment in the area reserved for the boxers, I noticed a solitary gentleman sitting cross-legged on the aerobics mat, doing nothing more than meditating. He had been in the lotus position for about 20 minutes already, and hadn't moved a muscle.

When he finally got up, he did so with a small but gentle spring in his step, as if he'd just had a good night's rest. What was he going to do next, I wondered. Go another round on the circuit machines? Or head straight to the showers? No, he walked briskly but calmly around the perimeters of the gym. And once he'd completed three laps, he returned straight to the aerobics mat. What was he going to do next? Surely, he wasn't going to meditate again? No, after quietly composing himself, he proceeded to do a round of stretching exercises, all of which took him about 20 minutes to complete.

For a moment, I was struck with awe and wonder because this was a man who was adhering to a fundamental principle of fitness training, never forgetting to slowly stretch his muscles before exerting them. No doubt, he would repeat this ritual after he completed his training.

How to Maintain Great Health

Watching this fine man, at peace with himself, led me to believe that he had achieved what is known as cognitive clarity. In Chapter 1, I provided you with an induction of what this entails, so I won't add any further detail for the time being. What I am going to do is remind you of what needs to be done to maintain that clarity. If you're in reasonably good mental and physical health, you won't require the assistance of a therapist or personal trainer.

What you will need is a routine that allows you to maintain your health. You don't need to exert yourself either. All you need to do is remember to keep yourself physically active (again, without overextending yourself), and maintain a healthy, balanced diet. Your work/life schedule needs to be well-maintained as well to ensure that you're never overwhelmed or collapse in a state of sheer exhaustion. Speaking of which, there is that other matter of sleep.

How to Train Your Brain

After a day that's been reasonably fulfilling, you should expect to feel tired during the early evening. This should give you every encouragement to go to bed early. A good night's rest for an equal amount of time every night is a fundamental requirement in terms of training your brain to remain calm and composed during other times of the day when you could expect to feel a little pressure.

No more noisy, late nights at the pub with the boys. Rather, a quiet evening of contemplation. Such an evening should never include hours of binge-watching your favorite TV shows. Rather, it should be devoted to keeping your mind fertile. For me personally, absorbing my mind in a couple of hours of reading works. But for other men, it could go as far as spending a little time in their workshops, keeping their hands busy as well.

Training your brain, as well as your body, doesn't require rocket science either. What it does require, however, is discipline, particularly if you've not yet acclimated to the health and wellness routine I'm alluding to. But sadly, for most men who don't appear to be able to bear the weight of the world on their shoulders with the calm and poise that is only idealized at this point of their lives, it remains to be seen.

It remains to be seen whether they'll have the patience to withstand just a few days of giving this new regime a tryout. That said, let me propose a little self-control.

How to Develop Self-Control

Just a little self-control will be enough to keep you out of trouble. Self-control is, however, a technique that will require time to develop. Bear with me while I show you how this can be done. My demonstration will also show that any work that you might need to do to self-adjust, doesn't need to intimidate you. It reminds me of the old adage: Less is more. Indeed, you'll be able to surprise yourself with the little you need to do to get going. After a few days and weeks of following a new routine, you won't mind the time spent ticking off your list.

In fact, you may well reach the stage where you'll want to do more. But therein lies a fundamental principle of better self-control. Make sure that you're getting enough rest. And make sure that you're taking enough breaks in between the tasks you've designated for yourself. This, however, does not mean rushing off to the pub at every opportunity you give yourself.

Begin your self-control development by starting small. Set small goals and reward yourself for completing them. During this time, you'll be giving yourself plenty of room to get to know yourself, and it's during this time that you're also allowed to be ambitious, thinking about longer-term goals that have always been on the back burner of what you believed was a chaotic life. During this time, you'll also surprise yourself after discovering that it will only require a few decisive decisions to change your life for the better.

Bearing in mind the immensity of this life-changing moment, and that self-control is designed to help control your behavior to avoid succumbing to unwanted urges or temptations, keep the following motivations in mind whenever you need to start thinking about the next month, with more to do but with fewer distractions:

- Always plan ahead, and continue exploring what you've learned about practicing self-control. Think of self-control as a disciplinary muscle that will get stronger the longer you continue developing it.

- When planning ahead, always focus on one goal at a time. Trying to do too much will only sap your existing willpower. It's like over-extending yourself during weight training and risking a debilitating injury. However, the ability to complete one goal will provide you with further motivation to take on a new, more challenging goal.

- Practice meditation. It's a great way to strengthen your self-control muscles. Meditation also teaches you to slow down and control impulses that might get in the way of your self-control.

- Always remind yourself of what could go wrong if you do nothing. Remind yourself always that self-control is a great confidence booster, and will benefit you in whatever area of life you're seeking to improve. It will also keep you healthy, fit, and well.

Impulse Control and Discipline

With greater self-control comes greater impulse control and discipline. It's interesting to note that psychology-based impulse control techniques were originally developed for people with attention deficit hyperactivity disorder (ADHD). As the disorder's name suggests, the techniques were designed for guys who couldn't pay attention and could never sit still, figuratively speaking of course. They could never focus on one thing at a time. Even so, you don't need to be diagnosed with an attention deficit disorder to see how the following approaches to your personal well-being could benefit you:

- I'd like to re-emphasize the need to ask for help when you're feeling mentally weak or overwhelmed. I'd like to remind you that there's no shame in asking others for help.

- Try your best to avoid situations that could trigger impulsive behavior. At the same time, work toward creating alternative but healthy outlets to satiate your impulsivity.

- While it never needs to be critical, consider how genetics or your current environment may have influenced the way you've become used to behaving.

- Take time out to learn new social skills, such as sharing, doing your fair share of work, and listening while others talk. When you've mastered these habits, you'll have completed another exercise in impulse control. It will also be a great motivation to help you develop new, healthy habits.

- Also, practice good timing. By this, I don't mean you're going to become a clock-watcher. What you are going to do is set a timer for the completion of designated tasks. Give yourself an estimate of how long it should take for you to complete your task. But when the timer goes off, stop what you're doing, and take a break.

Taking a break is feasible. It's not an exercise in laziness or complacency. It's a sensible habit well worth practicing. I've found it a useful habit to develop. Nevertheless, I won't lie to you about its challenges. Knowing that my break was drawing to a close, and the challenging task was looming, sometimes I could only let out a sigh of grief. In the beginning, I failed miserably at maintaining my disciplinary routine, easily tempted to call time on the rest of the day.

Be patient because developing discipline takes time, particularly if you've been lacking in this area of your life for a while. So, before I close this chapter with another challenge, let's talk about discipline.

In order to get by in life, we all need discipline. It's an inescapable fact of life we cannot escape from. Think about this for a moment: Imagine living your life completely lacking in discipline. Imagine that you have no support whatsoever to rely on that only encourages you to prolong a lazy, lackadaisical approach to life that allows you to do nothing or do as you please, while someone else does all the work. But even if that person was a glutton for punishment, they couldn't support you the entire way. For instance, do you honestly expect that they would be prepared to bathe you at night while you just sit there in the tub, staring into space?

I very much doubt it. Doing absolutely sweet nothing, with or without undeserved support, has its consequences. No job. No food. No roof over your head. No friends. No life. Well, there is a life you could look forward to: It's called a life on the streets. And when I say this, I mean absolutely no disrespect to those who have been forced onto the streets through circumstances they could not control. They deserve to be helped. You deserve better too, even though you're capable of doing so much more. But when you fail, don't run yourself down. Learn to forgive yourself, and move on with your life.

Before I end this section with a few more things you can do to lift yourself up out of the doldrums and go forward with your life, let me tell you what it takes to be disciplined. Discipline requires us to take personal responsibility for our actions or inactions. It is a soft skill that needs to be applied to different areas of our lives. Where it was lacking before, it now requires self-management. Simply put, it is like replacing a bad habit with a good one. Practically applied, discipline also teaches us to practice emotional self-regulation.

But proper discipline does not mean receiving a good beating for stepping out of line. Once you've come around to a rules-based routine that can help keep you out of trouble, you'll also appreciate how learning to discipline yourself will benefit you in the future. Apart from reducing stress and anxiety levels, self-discipline will make you a happier person. It will increase your ability to achieve both short- and long-term goals. In the context of this book's central theme, self-discipline will most certainly help you to keep your composure when you're faced with challenges that are part of everyday life. Apart from what I proposed earlier, you can do the following to help maintain your discipline as well:

- So that you don't forget them, always write down your goals.

- Prioritize both your goals and your daily tasks by creating a to-do list. This list will help keep you organized. It will also provide you with a great sense of accomplishment every time you've ticked off yet another completed task.

- Be mindful of your weaknesses. As incredible as this may seem, be willing to, quite literally, switch yourself off from them. Your first great step toward becoming self-disciplined is to acknowledge where you've been weak. The next step is to work toward changing your habits. But if you're struggling to switch yourself off from them, you can ask others to help switch you off from bad habits.

- Approach others to keep yourself accountable. Call on people you know and trust to help motivate you as well. But dump those who seem to derive enjoyment from running you down. It should be as clear as daylight that they have no interest in your self-improvement.

- It will become easier for you to switch yourself off from bad influences once you've changed your perspective on life. This is also a form of acceptance that teaches you to learn from your mistakes and motivate yourself to do better next time.

- For those times that you do stumble and fall, have a backup plan in place. For those times that you've failed, the backup plan will provide you with some breathing space to assess where you went wrong, and why you failed. It can also provide you with some material comfort that ties you over until such time that you're back on your feet.

Simply put, whether it's your fault or not is irrelevant when you've lost your job. You still need to find your next job, and that usually requires time and effort. It requires discipline too, of course. While you're out job-hunting with a similar sense of urgency that prehistoric men used when hunting for food, you can utilize what you've saved to pay your way. I know, saving for the proverbial rainy day has its challenges too, but for that, there's also help.

How to Handle Losing Composure

I fully understand that for men who have lost everything, the backup plan might be of little to no use. Having to make sweeping changes can be daunting and will always have its challenges. Whether it was their fault or not, men who have lost everything now need to dig deep to find new levels of resilience not previously experienced before. It's difficult enough to keep mind, body, and spirit together when there's nothing left in the tank. It's even more difficult for them to get back on their feet when there's no one out there to help them.

On that note, I'd like to underscore the importance of seeking help. Also, no matter how desperate your situation may be, positive results don't come overnight, no matter how much effort you've put into bringing this about, with or without the help of others. Patience is indeed a virtue, and when you're physically undernourished, it can be difficult to think clearly. This challenge could lead toward further irrationality that, consequently, makes things worse for you.

But let's be positive about this downward spiral. How much worse could things get? Right now, you might not be able to comprehend such a thought. I'm not going to encourage you to. I'm not even going to ask you to try and see the funny side of making mistakes or being knocked off your perch. That could be disrespectful. I can, however, ask you to take a deep breath. Give yourself a few moments before thinking about what you might be going through. But when you do so, try and be as honest as possible with yourself. Honesty will help provide the clarity you need. It will help you to see both the good and bad of what you're going through. While you're visualizing what a better life will look like for you, you can remind yourself of the worst of times.

Use this self-reflection to prepare yourself to bounce back. Use it well to regain some of your lost composure. But how to do this, you may be asking. Let me begin by asking you to reflect on what you've gained from your reading of this chapter. After all, you have already read a few strategies to develop composure in this book. Beginning with improved communication skills, the next chapter will continue with the build-up to what will constitute a fully composed, well-rounded, successful, and happy man.

In the meantime, let me provide you with a brief guide to use for so long. This guide focuses solely on what to do when you've completely lost it. It guides you on what to do when you've already lost your composure. I call it a survival guide for the time being. It's not a get-out-of-jail-free card, and it's not a bullet-proof contract that promises you a life-time guarantee. But it is a reasonable, rational magazine of bullets that can help to keep yourself safe and together for the time being.

Earlier, I began by suggesting that you stop what you're doing and take a deep breath. If you haven't yet done so, do so now. Also, treat yourself to what is commonly known as a cooling-off period. Not only is it a time to reflect on what happened, and what you did (or didn't do), but it's also a good time to reflect on what you said. But it's also a good time to reflect on what you didn't say.

This is an imperative that I've come to appreciate from my time working with the boys down at the gym. You see, it's all good and well to accept the cruel fate that life might have handed you. But what happens in life is usually at the behest of others. We all have the power, the ability, and the will, to change the course of life. And we should challenge those who didn't necessarily plot our downfall but did have a hand in it. Like us, they may have done and said things that shouldn't have been done and said and went on to cause harm to others. Worse still, and this has been a consequence of 21st-century life across the world, they may have done and said *nothing*.

After giving yourself a necessary pause, get back in the ring, and deal with the situation you're in. Keep the gloves on. There's no need to resort to being unreasonable, placing unrealistic demands on others who may have wronged you. Be patient because their day in court will come. You will still be required to speak out against wrongful actions that may have been committed against you, but before you do that, acknowledge where you may have been wrong, and if appropriate to do so, offer an apology. If you haven't already done so, make it clear to others, but especially to yourself, that you will be taking responsibility for your actions.

Make no mistake about it.

Now, before I close this chapter, let me quickly tell you a story about a not-so-young guy who almost lost it. Much, much older than them, he was different from many of the other guys that I've seen come and go through the doors of our gym. As a middle-aged man, he still hasn't met the woman of his dreams. In the gym's locker room, he hears a lot of talk among guys young enough to be his own sons about how they had a wild weekend with girls they met.

He couldn't contribute to the locker room talk. Self-conscious about his mature age, he was not only shy and lacking in confidence in the company of women, he was socially inadequate in front of men his own age as well. He also had a false impression of what his ideal woman should look like. He gave little thought to what she should *be* like. Initially intended as a means to stifle his loneliness and boredom over weekends, he started watching adult content. Of course, this weekend ritual soon developed into a nightly obsession, and it contributed horrendously toward a deterioration in his ability to communicate with women.

Communication, of course, is the next chapter's central theme. So, while I'm helping David to kill his porn addiction, and meet decent women his own age, I'll be introducing you to no less than three new characters whose personalities couldn't have been any less different. All three of them are key to the story I want to tell you about how to communicate like a self-assured gentleman with the utmost respect for not only the ladies but the gentlemen as well.

4. Communication

David is what you could call a socially awkward man. He never seems to fit in. Or at least, that's how he perceives himself. From what I've also gathered about his behavior in the last few months, is that he's too self-conscious about what others think of him. I have, however, tried to explain to him in the most subtle but most polite manner possible that nobody cares about you that much.

But I'm happy to tell you that David has stopped watching porn. As I did for you in the previous chapter, I introduced him to the importance of self-control and provided him with a few basic techniques he could use to get himself off this unfortunate, self-destructive habit. For instance, he took the radical step of cutting himself off from the Wi-Fi privileges his apartment complex offered him. He also spends less time at the gym. That's because he has met new friends through the support group he joined after disconnecting himself from his self-destructive habit.

No, David's not mixing with like-minded souls who are still struggling to come to terms with their lack of sexual prowess. After learning with some incredulity that women can also fall foul of the lure of pornography, he found it just a little easier to engage with them about mutually shared weaknesses. Coffee shop discussions soon blossomed into coffee shop romances. Moments of discovery in the group therapy sessions were shared. These had little to do with their awareness of their low self-esteem. Rather, it had everything to do with how others responded to their overtures.

Not by any stretch of the imagination were these tacky one-liners that went out of fashion during the 80s. More so, they were sincere wishes that others may have a good day.

Whether over the phone during a business call or in the supermarket checkout line, wishing the person opposite you a good day has become a permanent part of our vocabulary. Well, for most of us, it has been the case. I cannot say when this good habit started but I sometimes wonder what happened in the intervening years. Twenty years into the new millennium, things seem to have gotten worse. The way people talk to each other has become a sound for sore ears. No, it's not so much that the respect for others who are distinctly different from us has diminished, it's more a case of how quickly our social mores have changed over the years since the millennium bug was squashed. Call me old-fashioned but I blame the internet and the social media networks that piggy-back on it.

Let me set aside the blame game for now, and introduce you to three interesting characters. Because *The Art of Composure* is primarily a book written for men about men, these characters have to be men as well. Never mind David, but Jack personifies the quintessentially 21st-century socially awkward male. Being a millennial himself, you would have thought that he'd fit in with the rest of the crowd, like a pair of well-worn gloves. But no.

By the way, there's nothing wrong with being an introvert, being such a character myself. But in this story, I'm the narrator, so let me also tell you the story about Bob, a confident introvert not yet in his prime but certainly making heads turn in more ways than one, mostly for all the right reasons. Bob's story is a wag in the tail that proves that there are advantages to being a confident introvert. Don't worry too much about Jack because like you, I'm helping him too.

It turns out that I don't need to help Ron. You see, Ron's perfectly capable of standing on his own two feet. He is what we call the smooth operator but in this case, not in a bad way. Unlike most of the guys he hangs out with, he gets his way with women. But what makes him stand out from the rest of the crowd is that he knows how to treat them as well.

Apart from Jack, Bob and Ron are well-versed in the art of effective communication. It's not communications 101, just a basic set of rules that have stood the test of time. Introducing you to these rules, I'm also going to show you how to apply composure to the way you communicate with others, both men and women.

The Socially Awkward

Let me introduce you to Jack. Sometimes, when he's out and about downtown, he sticks out like a sore thumb. People have noticed. He seems to have noticed too. In fact, he's quite subconscious about it but is clueless as to what to do about his lack of social adequacy. I have noticed too. Jack comes to the gym sometimes, and boy, do the boys notice this socially awkward young man.

Fortunately, they are more focused on their own training, and most of them don't give him the time of day. I said that it was fortunate that poor Jack was being ignored for the time being because I have concerns about bullying. My young men have been taught well to not lower themselves to this form of behavior but unfortunately, when testosterone levels are raging in the ring or on the side, down in the weights and circuit training galleys, anything could happen.

Not that anything should happen because poor Jack does his level best to stay out of sight. If he shows up at all, he spends most of his time ducking the medicine ball or patting the punching bag as if it's his long-lost furry pal on four legs.

Even though poor Jack is afraid of people, his bark remains worse than his bite. Come to think of it, while this thin 24-year-old coat-hanger of a young man is prone to losing his temper when pressured into a corner, he can hardly hurt a fly. But because time flies as well, I need to describe what constitutes a socially awkward person.

If you're socially awkward, you might be completely out of your depth, and certainly uncomfortable in social situations. At any given time, if you were called to the center of the room at a party, you might cause the death of the party. Seriously though, being asked (or demanded) to be the center of attraction is not only awkward, it's downright unpleasant.

And if a person is socially afflicted, it could be because he's suffering from extreme anxiety. It's not unusual to be in this situation. In fact, the National Institute of Mental Health (NIMH) reports that up to 12% of adults in the United States will experience a social anxiety disorder at some stage of their lives. Finally, visible signs that you might be socially awkward, could be manifested by any one or more of the following:

- Avoiding eye contact.

- Fidgeting, sweating, and feeling anxious.

- Unable to read body language, you also have difficulty talking.

- You're always feeling self-conscious and probably wondering what others are thinking or saying about you.

Of course, socially awkward people are inherently poor communicators, whether in a crowd or in one-on-one situations, it makes no difference. In the extreme, a socially awkward person could be suffering from a social communication disorder. Someone who is clinically diagnosed with this disorder, will not only have verbal communication difficulties, but non-verbal challenges as well. Language processing difficulties are not far off the mark for a socially inadequate person either.

Here, I'm focusing primarily on speaking skills. Or in this unfortunate case, the lack thereof. Indeed, verbal communication difficulties are characterized by the following downsides:

- Greeting other people inappropriately.

- Never giving others a chance to speak, the socially inadequate person may be prone to talking over the heads of others.

- Alongside inappropriate body language, inappropriate verbal language is used as well.

- Stories are told in a disjointed manner, and the socially anxious person is usually unable to stay on topic.

- Even if he's an inherently decent person, the socially awkward person may even resort to using foul, offensive, inappropriate, indecent language, or excessive language.

Dealing With Social Anxiety

A person who's been diagnosed with social anxiety disorder, also known as social phobia, could be suffering from a medical condition that causes fear and anxiety whenever he's around people in social situations. As a socially anxious person, he fears being judged or watched by others.

Apart from not wanting to perform or speak in front of people, the socially anxious person even finds it difficult to eat in front of people. He could even have a fear of using restrooms as well. Social anxiety isn't confined to group situations. Tragically, the socially anxious person doesn't like taking or making phone calls, and no matter how good his qualifications or credentials are, he's going to have a hard time participating in a job interview, particularly since he's going to be expected to answer questions.

Someone who has a social phobia like Jack can forget about dating for the foreseeable future. But should his condition ever be diagnosed as chronic, it's good to know that there's treatment available for him. Apart from being prescribed antidepressants, it's ironic to note that a favored therapy for someone in his condition is talk therapy.

Socially Awkward Situations

In order for an accurate diagnosis to be completed, Jack's therapist will be referring to the American Psychiatric Association's (APA) Diagnostic and Statistical Manual of Mental Disorders (DSM-5). For Jack to be positively diagnosed, he would have to experience one or more of the following criteria:

- Experience ongoing intense fear or anxiety about social conditions because of a fear of being judged or humiliated.

- Avoid social situations that may cause anxiety.

- Experience intense anxiety that could be out of proportion to the situation being encountered.

- Fear or anxiety of social situations interferes with day-to-day life.

- The fear or anxiety cannot be explained by a medical condition. Medication, prescribed or not, and even substance abuse, cannot be blamed for this disorder.

Even so, I think it's commendable, probably even brave, that Jack continues to show up for practice at least three times a week. I've excused him from the missed days because I've begun to appreciate what he might be going through. I'm not yet ready to propose one-on-one training for him after hours. I believe he has much more progress to make before he reaches that stage.

The Confident Introvert

Let me introduce you to Bob. He can relate to poor Jack because he's been where the thin young man is. But if I may be so bold as to pat me and my fellow trainers on the backs, coming to the gym has helped Bob emerge from the shadows. Not only has he developed fine, nicely refined muscles, but he's also developed both a spine and thick skin as well. He doesn't take what others say lightly, nor as the case may be, does he always take what others say with a pinch of salt.

Bob has developed enough self-confidence to take care of himself and to protect himself at night while making his way through some of the dark, dodgy streets from the gym to his apartment late at night. Why he chooses to stay so late at night is beyond me. It's not as though he has no life and has nowhere to go. Then again, it could have something to do with him balancing his life out with other priorities during the day.

Bob knows how to talk to people. He also knows how to listen to people but stops short of trying to give them too much advice. As far as he's concerned, if he wanted to lecture them, he would have become a lecturer down at the community college four blocks away from our building.

By now, Bob knows how to compose himself in uncomfortable situations. Apart from choosing late-night routes, he also knows how to avoid such situations. Not that he's deliberately seeking to avoid them, it's just that he likes to keep himself prepared. Unlike Jack, he doesn't have any social anxiety hang-ups to worry about. He addressed that a long time ago, since the first day he walked into our gym, shoulders sagging, and waistline paunch showing.

Today, however, with shoulders back and a trim waistline second to none, Bob is a completely different picture of health. While he's got a good fashion sense, he dresses fairly modestly, not wishing to draw attention to himself. Whether at the gym or at college, Bob's proud of his achievements but is not, as they say, proud as a peacock. Bob prefers to keep a low profile.

Bob remains mindful of his own vulnerabilities as a young man still trying to make his way in the world, and would much rather that he didn't get invited into crowded, late-night weekend situations. Sensibly, he's always managed to utilize a little diplomacy, inventively telling the odd white lie here and there, so as not to hurt or offend. Not that I'm condoning dishonesty, but I have observed that Bob has developed his own set of coping mechanisms to help him out of social situations that make him feel uncomfortable.

But I have to mention that even though he'd prefer to keep a low profile, and out of trouble, he's one of the first to rush to poor Jack's defense, if necessary.

So, how can one define Bob? How does one describe what is known as a confident introvert? If you're a fan of movies like I am, you'll know that Will Smith, the Academy Award-winning actor who, once upon a time in LA, slapped the lights out of comedian Chris Rock, like Ali he portrayed in a movie of the same name, is not a confident introvert. Sometimes, I think Smith talks too much.

A better example would, of course, be Clint Eastwood's gun-toting loner, hiding behind his poncho and wide-brimmed hat in *The Good, The Bad, and The Ugly*. Seriously, though, you've got a lot going for you if you are what they call a confident introvert. While you still prefer quiet corners, the following positive characteristics could be attributed to you:

- Preferring to be alone, you might be in your element in terms of being productive and creative.

- You'd like to go beyond meaningless small talk and engage in deep and meaningful conversations.

Philosophical discussions about life, hopes, dreams, and fears are never beyond you.

- You're more than capable of holding your own, standing on your own two feet, and making independent decisions. Once you've drawn your own conclusions, you do feel a sense of empowerment but never a sense of entitlement that suggests that you're right while the other is wrong.

After all, as an independent thinker and thought-provoker, you'd still like to hear what the other has to say.

How to Demonstrate Composure in Uncomfortable Situations

You don't need to be socially awkward like Jack is to feel uncomfortable. Particularly when you're under pressure from work or in your relationship with a woman you're going out with, you could easily drop your guard, ending up saying or doing the wrong things and later coming to regret it. So, to avoid this happening to you, let's provide you with a demonstration of composure.

It's probably the most important thing you need to do in an uncomfortable situation. Whether you're confronted with a bout of shyness in front of the most beautiful woman you've ever met or nervous tension in front of a hard but not unreasonable taskmaster at work, the best thing you can do for yourself is to just be yourself. Before, during, and after placing yourself in the firing line, make sure you've gotten in the habit of monitoring your body language to the point that it's become natural for you.

So natural that hardly anyone's noticed. While you need to be sincere about your intentions toward your opposite number or someone of interest to you, you need to remain mindful of your boundaries. Not in a bad way but as a socially limited person, you need to show others that you're able to keep your cool. More importantly, you need to show yourself that you've got what it takes to turn a situation around, never mind what the other person is thinking.

More than likely, it's not what he's thinking that matters. And you never know, maybe she hasn't even noticed the tiny string of spinach stuck between your gleaming white teeth, always regularly brushed, just like your mother taught you.

The Smooth Operator

Let me introduce you to Ron. Black, white, Latino, or Asian, I couldn't help noticing how some of the other guys grew green with envy. In terms of muscles, speed between the ropes, and basic fitness levels, he's not exactly heads and shoulders above the rest of the young men. Come to think of it, he's no marvel in the looks department either. So why would the other chaps envy him? Well, on those rare occasions that the ladies do show up for training, Ron never hesitates to get a word in with them.

Not one but all of them have a tendency to thrust themselves at his feet whenever he shows up. I'm not exaggerating. He seems to have a way with women, and whether they're introverts or not, I am sure many men may wonder just how he does it. As a certified boxing trainer and a part-time employee at the gym, I have no business asking him anyway. I'm not entitled to choose pickup lines among the customers if you will.

It's just a rumor, but so I've heard: Customer relations are a forte of Ron's as well. He does really well in the presence of others. But never seeks to dominate the crowd. He might be the most outrageously cool guy I've come across for a long time but he doesn't strike me as someone who's deliberately seeking attention.

Even so, he's still a smooth operator. Let me explain why. Like most men, me included, he enjoys the company of women. But unlike many men, he seems to have no difficulty in striking up a conversation with the opposite sex. It's not as though he's oozing in charisma with sexual pheromones added in, he just seems to know how to talk to them. Ron relates with women as if he was one of them.

No, it's not that either, but boy, does this distinguished gentleman have charm! He's certainly fun to be around, even the guys say so. He also has an opinion about everything under the sun but his capacity for emotional intelligence ensures that he never gets under anyone's skin. I think it's important to mention that he doesn't need to use his muscles to defend himself. He can get by with his words, and he's even prepared to stick his neck out for others, particularly poor Jack.

But before you get any ideas about how to conduct yourself with women, let me remind you of how *not* to behave when in the company of women. Particularly in the workplace, and certainly not during training at the gym, entertain no romantic illusions with the opposite sex. That keeps you from curbing your enthusiasm when engaging in conversations with women. When you do speak to a woman, be careful how you use your hand gestures and do not—I repeat—do not touch her person.

Being gay doesn't excuse you either, and as far as I'm concerned, gay men, particularly since they're still men, are just as capable of falling into the sexism trap as so-called straight men. While men are men, women are still women. Treat them accordingly. You're allowed to politely smile while speaking to a woman but be careful of how you use humor in order to avoid the sexist trap.

Particularly in the workplace, don't make it obvious that your female colleague is a woman, and never, never assume that because she's a woman, she's not up to the job. Apart from her charming but unique personality, don't ever make it obvious that because of her gender, she's inherently different from you.

Stand Tall, Look Them in the Eye, and Use Your Hands if You Have To

But there are times when it's necessary to stand tall, look them in the eye, and use your hands if you need to. Not to touch them, mind you but just as the Italians do. Italian men and women, generally speaking, are extremely expressive when exploiting their garrulous nature. They're so talkative that you'd begin to wonder: Why use hand gestures at all?

Whether you're in the company of women or men or both, it's important that you stand tall physically, with your back straight and shoulders back. This shows that you're confident in the company of others, and in moments of confrontation, won't be too bothered by what your opponent is trying to communicate, other than attempting to correct his behavior, if appropriate to do so.

Benefits of Being Outgoing

You've got a number of things going for you if you're an outgoing person. But what constitutes an outgoing person? An outgoing person can be the life of the party. Not only that, he tends to enjoy being in the limelight. It doesn't have to be a disadvantage and can be used as a form of upliftment for others who are hesitant. An outgoing person loves having a conversation. More importantly, perhaps, he could have a number of fine qualities that make him a great leader.

If you were ever to materialize as an extrovert, what sort of benefits could you expect to look forward to? All within reason, I think the following features characterize Ron well:

- Ron is a team player and enjoys working in a group.

- As an extrovert, he's more than happy to open up and discuss problems, if and when they arise.

- As a born leader, the extrovert doesn't take long to make a connection with people. He doesn't need to judge them but can sum them up fairly quickly.

- Surprisingly, an extrovert acts before thinking. Acting out in the heat of the moment could be an advantage, particularly when both Ron and his pals are threatened.

Basic Rules for Communication

Even when you're totally confident in your ability to handle social situations, you still need to remind yourself to observe basic rules of social etiquette. Such rules allow you to enjoy the favor of others, particularly during stressful times. At the same time, you still need to be able to assert yourself without causing offense. You're entitled to let others know where you stand, how you're feeling, and what you require from them if needs be. This is important to help you avoid trying to please all people, at the same time. Trying to do so is virtually impossible, and will only cause you more unnecessary stress, no matter how hard you try.

Good communication skills entail having the skillful ability to use your voice to the best effect without ever having to raise it. Moreover, both you and those you converse with will feel comfortable if you're able to masterfully project yourself physically. Finally, no matter who you're with, and no matter what you say, it remains important that you show respect. In your case, let respect be earned, and if someone chooses to ignore the courtesy you extend to him, then it's on him.

Importance of Good Communication Skills

Without good communication skills, you could find yourself in no-man's land. It will be like living on an island, and you're the only human being on the island. Not a living soul to talk to. In reality, when you communicate with others, it sometimes feels as though no one's listening to you. And if they are, they aren't taking you seriously. To turn this sense of isolation around, all you need to do is learn to observe and practice the basics of good communication skills. Once you've done that, you'll soon see how you're able to enjoy the following benefits of good communication skills:

- Trust

- Respect

- Problem-solving

- Overcome differences

- Share ideas

To my mind, nothing is more reassuring than being trusted and being able to trust others. Also, I've learned to overcome the differences of others by learning to respect them. But the way I've learned to listen to them, and project myself toward them, has helped me to gain their respect.

Importance of Body Language

Never mind what you have to say, it's your body language or nonverbal cues that could make all the difference in helping you secure a sought-after career position. Or the woman of your dreams, someone you'd feel comfortable with, living on an idyllic island with nothing but palm trees, smooth white sand, and pale blue sea water to keep you company.

Your prospective employer needs reassurance that he'll be able to trust you in your new position. And your new girlfriend needs to feel safe with you, particularly when you're able to look her in the eye with sincerity. She also needs to see that you're comfortable with yourself and that there's no tension or confusion in the way you present yourself to her. Finally, the following three factors are crucial in your ability to better manage your body language:

- Learn to manage your stress levels in the moment. When you get stressed or uncomfortable, it is important that you don't show it because showing it only adds to the fire. A few ways to manage your stress include controlling your breathing by slowing it down to 4 counts of inhales and exhales. Focus on relaxing your shoulders, by doing this you'll also be less likely to fidget. Finally, your stress levels can become unmanageable at times, if so take a break from the situation you're in, excuse yourself politely and find a quiet place, this is a much more composed alternative to displaying anger, nervousness or other negative emotions.

- Develop your emotional awareness abilities. Doing so also helps you to read the body language of others. You need to be aware of your emotions so that you can carry out the correct coping mechanism straight away to maintain composure. A simple way to do this is to get into the habit of pausing before reacting, it doesn't have to be a 5 second pause like you have a bad internet connection on a video call, take 1 second to think about what you have encountered, pair an emotion with it and continue.

- Your ability to be an expert in reading body language negates the need to become a mind reader. It also trains you to have confidence in your instincts. The more conversations you have with different people the better you become at reading body language. Some tips to help you include observing their posture, hand gestures, facial expressions, eye contact (but avoid having staring contests), personal space and overall body tension. Keeping an eye out for these signals helps you grasp what they are actually thinking and feeling.

Slowing Down

Many composed characters in films throughout the years, whether good or bad, tend to display their ability to handle pressure by communicating at a slow pace. For example Vito Corleone in The Godfather (1972), played by Marlon Brando. Vito's speech is famously slow and measured, never rushed or impulsive. This deliberate pace makes him a compelling and authoritative figure. In one of the most iconic scenes, when he says, "I'm gonna make him an offer he can't refuse," the calmness and control in his voice heighten the intensity of his message. His slow delivery gives weight to every word, making him seem more powerful and in control, even in high-stakes situations.

Sounding like a gangster from the 1970s may not be best suited for you, especially when speaking about what you are having for dinner. Slowing down, however, is a simple and great technique to apply to your communication when you feel yourself getting stressed or nervous. It is important that you are able to identify when you lose composure because that is when you can flick the little switch in your head to slow down and regain your composure. We can lose composure at any moment, so when you feel signs of stress or nervousness follow the tips below to help yourself slow down:

- Practice mindful breathing: Before speaking, take a deep breath to center yourself. Throughout the conversation, pay attention to your breathing and take pauses to inhale slowly. This naturally slows down your pace and helps you feel more in control.

- Use pauses effectively: After making a point, pause for a moment before continuing. This not only slows down your speech but also creates an opportunity for the listener to digest your words. Don't be afraid of silence.

- Focus on articulation: Pay attention to how you pronounce each word. Rather than rushing through sentences, take your time to fully pronounce words and enunciate clearly. This helps ensure your message is understood.

- Be conscious of your tone and volume: Speak in a calm, measured tone, and keep your volume steady. Slower communication tends to have a more soothing, confident effect, while speaking too quickly can sound anxious or aggressive.

- Limit multitasking: Focus solely on the conversation at hand. Whether it's a face-to-face talk or a phone call, give it your full attention. This will allow you to slow down, think carefully about your responses, and avoid distractions.

- Break your thoughts into segments: Break your thoughts into smaller, more manageable segments. Communicate one idea at a time, then pause to let the listener digest it before moving on to the next point.

- Be mindful of non-verbal cues: Pay attention to your body language and that of others. For instance, if the listener looks confused or hasn't had a chance to

143

respond, it may be a sign that you're speaking too quickly. Slow down, allow pauses, and invite feedback with open body language.

Slowing down improves your clarity, thoughtfulness, encourages active listening and makes you feel more confident in uncomfortable situations. It takes time to get the hang of slowing down, with practice you will get there. Make a start by practicing on your own and start applying the techniques to low intensity situations, eventually you can work your way up to communication situations you find intense and keep this technique ready to use as a coping strategy.

Importance of Active Listening Skills and How to Use Them

Never mind being a good listener, what does it take to be an active listener? It's great that someone knows that you're listening. But wouldn't it be even better to start activating more intentional, and more meaningful conversations, just like the confident introvert is able to do? To help you get this much right in future conversations, observe the following rules:

- Be fully present in the conversation.

- Show intent and interest by maintaining good eye contact.

- Use non-verbal cues while at the same time paying attention to those of your fellow-communicant.

- Listen to understand rather than to respond.

- When responding, ask open-ended questions to encourage further responses.

- To show that you've heard every word that was said, paraphrase, and reflect back on what was said.

Showing Respect

The importance of showing others respect cannot be emphasized more. It doesn't matter who you're addressing. It doesn't matter what age or gender that person is either. Earlier, I spoke about how we should treat a lady. When you met her for the first time, she might not have regarded herself as such. It's your task to turn on the charm and make her feel that she is indeed a lady. But when you do this, don't get too carried away with the stereotypical chivalry that's been attributed to us.

Not only does the lady want to feel respect, but she also wants to be treated as your equal. Finally, I'd like to talk about an area that might come across as being contentious for old-fashioned parents. Fathers, in general, like to show their kids that they're still the men of the house. That's all good and well. But at the same time, I like to make younger men feel comfortable in my presence.

While I certainly don't want to be treated as an old man (and I'm not!), I want them to feel that I'm their friend. While I want to feel comfortable in the company of others, particularly if they're culturally different from me, I want them to feel comfortable with me as well. I think that by showing enough composure in the company of others, particularly when conversing with them, you're not only making them feel comfortable, you're going to feel comfortable too.

Not only are you comfortable with others, you're comfortable with yourself. So much so that you wouldn't want to change anything about yourself, not for the world. Well, there's always room for improvement. While things change, people change too.

Applying Composure to Communication

David has finally killed his porn habit! You'll agree that this is good news. Also, he's composed himself enough to switch the Wi-Fi back on in his apartment. He's taught himself enough impulse control to feel confident that he's not going to fall back into temptation again. At the same time, he's mature enough to accept that, particularly during stressful times of the year, there might be occasions where he could suffer a relapse.

Thankfully, that hasn't happened yet. But David knows that should a relapse ever occur, he's got more than enough support to help him overcome his ordeal. I'm happy to say that David's also spending more time at the gym. Yes, he's become more acutely aware of his age and wants very much to keep himself fit and healthy. He also wants to be happy, and in accordance with a man's need to be in the company of others, he's decided to pay closer attention to his appearance.

David is more comfortable in his own skin. There's hardly a shred of fat around his waistline, but that's not the point. David's comfortable with who he is as a man, completely *au fait* with his unique personality. He's made a smooth transition from being a socially awkward, middle-aged man, aging before his time, to a confident introvert, comfortably getting along with everyone that crosses his path.

Asking David to become a smooth operator is asking too much. He doesn't want to draw too much attention to himself and is quite happy to bide his time making new friends and acquaintances on the side. David is not about to get carried away with the positive changes he's made to his life. He's less inclined to talk to every Dick, Tom, and Harry, and maybe Martha too, and more inclined to talk to someone with the mind of a Dickens or Einstein. In no hurry to make new friends, David is focusing on quality rather than quantity. He is patient enough to know that good, quality friends won't be falling from the sky like manna from heaven, no matter how fervently you want something like this to happen, and no matter how hard you work at making new friends.

Get a Life

Not only do you want to get a life (come to think of it, you might already *have* a life), you want to show others that this is your intent. You want them to notice the changes in you. But unlike Ron, our resident Smooth Operator, you don't want to make it *that* obvious.

In the context of this motivation, not wanting to draw attention to yourself is not the same as being shy, introverted, or socially inept. It's more in tune with you being comfortable with who you are and what you'd like to do to improve yourself. But in the context of this chapter, the way you project yourself to others allows them to notice you in a positive, complimentary way. Rather than bowing their heads to listen to every opinion you insist on voicing, others are relieved to notice that you're listening to them. You're making them feel comfortable in their own skin as well, and you're happy to wait your turn before responding in conversations.

Appearance Always Matters

Good to know that you've addressed your body language. Or verbal cues. Even better that you've reminded yourself that a confident, respectful posture counts for nothing if you've done nothing about your appearance.

Previously, I used to take the line that it doesn't matter what others think of me. It doesn't matter what they think about how I dress. What mattered more to me was being comfortable in the clothes I wore. Of course, it matters how you appear to others. And it's not just about respecting them, it's about respecting yourself.

Remind Yourself That You're in Control

You don't need to be a bully to remind others that you're in charge. It's more important to remind *yourself* that *you're* in control. You're in control of your life. You're in control of your circumstances. And in the context of this motivation, you're in control of the story.

Being in control of the conversation doesn't mean that you're going to dominate it. If needs be, there are more subtle ways to get your message across, particularly if your conversationalist turns out to be an antagonist. You can see his aggression from a mile off, never mind hearing it in his voice. When you step forward confidently to reprimand or block your aggressor, your voice is pitched loud enough to be heard. There's no need for you to be aggressive like your antagonist. If your voice is firm and authoritative, he will get the message you're attempting to project. Also, your body language is relaxed and composed enough to show him that you're not afraid of him. You've also planted the thought in his mind that you're probably ready to deal with a strike from him if it comes to that.

When You Need to Take a Step Back

Sometimes, I like to keep a low profile. But it's not the same as hiding under the covers so that no one knows you're there. In order to remain composed, you need to maintain your presence. You don't need to raise your voice to let others know that you're still in the room and can still hear every word they're saying. If you've observed all of the above suggestions for good communication, they'll know you're still with them.

But yes, it's nice. It's nice to keep a low profile every once in a while. It's soothing to be able to take a breather from the conversation to give yourself a break. If you operate like Ron, the Smooth Operator, it can be exhausting. But what's richly rewarding about taking a step back and letting others dominate the room for a while, is that not only is your self-confidence intact, you're also giving others, particularly those who are less fortunate than you, a chance to elevate their self-esteem.

Never Mind What Others Think

Whether in a conflict situation or holding your own during a dialogue exchange that's both stimulating and intriguing, it's important that you keep on standing tall. You're not going to mind what others think of you. It's on them if they think otherwise of you. After all, you're doing your level best to lift yourself up to not only be the man you always wanted to be but to be a decent man as well.

It's not even a case of playing it safe when you say or do the right thing. In this context, playing it safe means saying or doing the things that others want. What matters to them does count but always remember that what matters to you should count in equal measure as well. Just as long as you're honest with yourself (and toward others without any need to be abrupt or abrasive in your choice of vocabulary), it shouldn't matter what others think of you.

Always Challenge Yourself

Always challenge yourself to be better than you were yesterday. More importantly, challenge your thoughts and words. There's no need to be pretentious and make a fool of yourself using words, phrases, or expressions that you don't fully comprehend. Chances are that they won't understand a word you're saying either. But chances are that there could be someone in the room who knows.

He knows that you're not being sincere. He knows that you're trying to do too much (it's not necessary) to better yourself in front of others. Rather, challenge yourself to be honest and sincere, and don't let false impressions come back to bite you.

Sometimes, you're allowed to sweat it out in the room when it's become a pressure cooker of conflicts, mixed emotions, and disagreements. But I think it would be a whole lot better if you can just compose yourself. Remember, composing yourself doesn't need to happen in the moment. Great composure in communication settings, particularly if they're challenging, can take place behind the scenes. That's to say that before entering a room and engaging yourself with others, you've allowed yourself plenty of room to prepare.

Good preparation before the event is not a form of insincerity. It's common sense and also shows that you're a mature thinker. You're sensible, but you're also kind and considerate. You take care of your emotions, but you're also respectful of what others need to say. Good preparation before engaging in an important conversation or a conversation that cannot be avoided will help you immeasurably when you're lacking in confidence. When you're lacking confidence, you're usually thinking negatively.

And when you're thinking negatively, you can challenge your negativity too. Sadly, negativity comes across in the conversations you're having with others. So, before your next important conversation, let's attempt to address the self-doubt that might be a contributing factor toward your lack of composure in tight situations.

When I talk about challenging negativity, I'm sometimes reminded of the story I told you at the beginning of this book. Back then, I was comparing how we've changed over thousands of years. Back then, it was only natural to be scanning the horizon for threats. Looking out for perceived and actual threats has always been a sign of survival. But even today, this natural preoccupation with threats, rather than maintaining physical and emotional safety, could do more harm than good.

Even so, it's always possible to overturn negative thoughts. It turns out that this positive action is a natural, human response as well. By challenging your negative thoughts, you're reframing your tendency to negative self-talk. By challenging your negative self-talk, you're not only telling yourself that you're going to do better but that you *will* do better. Of course, there's work to do in this area. That said, the following actions should help you to shift the way you're thinking:

- **Cultivate self-awareness**: In order to begin the process of challenging the natural inclination to have negative thoughts, you need to become fully aware that you're having them. You also need to make yourself aware of *when* you're saying such negative things about yourself or your circumstances. Finally, a better understanding of the triggers that cause you to say what you're saying, and why you're saying it, contributes toward the required levels of self-awareness needed to challenge negative thoughts.

- **Challenge the thought**: An effective challenge is to search for evidence that disproves the negative thoughts you're having. Once you have your evidence, you can challenge your negative thoughts using the evidence to reaffirm your capabilities and increase your confidence levels.

- **Practice self-love**: This ability is necessary if you want to overcome your negative thinking habit. Practicing self-love allows you to fully accept who you are as a man, also accepting that you're not perfect. Loving yourself allows you to respect yourself, providing yourself with a sense of insistence that you're not going to address yourself in ways that have kept you back from achieving your best.

In the meantime, Jack still needs to address his social phobia issues. What can we do to help him emerge from his shell? What can we do to make him realize that he's more worthy than he thinks he is?

When I first had a one-on-one with Jack about his social phobia, I made the suggestion that he should practice being out in the open. Even on those days, he didn't feel comfortable being out there. He would also need to practice speaking in public. When I told him this, and more, Jack nearly fell off his chair. Impossible! his negative self-talk seemed to be telling him. But I could only retort: Nothing's impossible Jack. Things only seem impossible until it's done.

Even so, it was easier said than done. I wasn't Jack's therapist, and I couldn't force him into things he didn't want to do. But as a certified gym instructor, I had every right to tell him that he needed to relax. If not, he would need to start practicing relaxation techniques. After all, if his muscles were tense while trying to workout on the circuit machines, he'd be setting himself up for an injury. Doing stretching exercises before exerting himself would also help to keep his muscles relaxed.

All things being equal, Jack needed to stop comparing himself with others. He needed to start saying nice things about himself. And if keeping himself out of the spotlight for a while longer was going to help him, then so be it. After all, I had to concede that Jack's road to recovery would require him to do things that bring him comfort. No more than that could I do.

Even so, I could relate to what Jack was going through. Like me, Jack was someone who hated conflict. I asked myself once whether Jack suffered some childhood trauma. Was Jack one of those nimble young boys trying his utmost best to hide away on the school playground to avoid being bullied? I had my fair share of bullying as a kid, so I know what that might feel like. I've also had enough of it. Perhaps you have too. Rest assured that bullying is being dealt with in all areas of life.

But conflict, by and large, has its own set of complexities. Conflict is not something we can hide from. It's not something we can run away from either. It's a fact of life, and it needs to be challenged head-on. Believing that we can tackle it like a beefy cornerback in a college football team, we know this much about conflict: You don't need a helmet to deal with it. You don't even need a pair of boxing gloves. Body language and strong vocal skills will make a huge difference. But going from being a regular pushover to a champion takes time. We'll talk about this in the next chapter.

5. Navigating Conflict with Composure

Charles was being made fun of again. John kept calling Charles a posh twat and taking his lunch money off him in the canteen. It was not Charles' fault that he spoke well. Certainly, his English language skills were a lot more advanced than that of the other boys on the school playground. It was hardly his fault that he went over and above what was required of him at the language-learning level pertaining to his grade. Charles loved reading. So much so that his concerned parents hardly needed to provide him with any encouragement.

They had no concerns about Charles' capacity for reading and writing. They had concerns about the number of times he was coming home after school with bruises, knowing full well that as a mild-mannered, studious introvert, he didn't cause the fight. More was to come by the time they finally secured an appointment to see the school principal. It almost boiled down to an argument, and not comfortable in the arts of conflict resolution. Charles' parents had to accept the misguided advice from the principal that he had to learn how to tough it out just like all the other boys.

Later that night, Charles did some internet research. He was looking for methods of composure to help both him and his parents deal with conflict. He also wanted to learn how to negotiate but set aside any notion of winning a conflict for now. He didn't want to look too far ahead. Even so, he was still hopeful. Of the following five conflict resolution techniques he highlighted, he believed that he had a better than even chance of meeting at least three of them:

- Avoidance

- Accommodation

- Compromise

- Collaboration

- Competition

Charles would have been more than happy to do everything in his power to avoid a potential conflict altogether. But that would have been easier said than done, so for the time being, he resorted to rolling with the punches and backing himself into a compromising corner, until such time that he could learn the arts of negotiation that would, no doubt, be required to triumph in a conflict situation.

In the meantime, Charles flipped through his dictionary to find a comprehensive definition of conflict. The schoolyard bullying incident was one such example but Charles wanted to dig a little further to find more examples of conflict since the beginning of mankind. All he could think of was that since the beginning of time, wars were fought over who knows how many territorial disputes. In fact, there were no less than two world wars during the previous century. But after World War II ended, divorce rates climbed as folks adjusted to becoming what became known as the nuclear family.

Today, bullying and many forms of discrimination are being challenged, even in some of the country's highest courts. But where agreements could be reached, the people party to those agreements may already have had a grasp of what conflict is. You see, in Charles' estimation, a conflict boils down to a set of unacceptable differences in interests, values, and opinions between individuals and groups.

While there was no chance of that happening under Charles' roof, sometimes it's inevitable. Sometimes it's necessary. Folks get divorced because all love is lost, and there are irreconcilable differences. Sometimes, there's even abuse. People also get into arguments over property issues, and if their arguments don't land in court, as they probably should, violence and vandalism could occur. Astoundingly, this is what happens within what is supposed to be a civil society.

Apart from bullying and disagreements over property rights, conflict arises because of differences in opinion, leadership differences, and management styles, as well as misunderstandings between people who haven't come to terms with their differences. If it gets any worse than that, people could be filing discrimination suits in a court of law. They know this much about civil society today. It may be riddled with holes but those who are oppressed or abused by conflict, have rights.

And they can fight back.

Fighting back doesn't mean climbing into a boxing ring like Ali did against Spinks in the late 70s. It doesn't mean challenging your opponent to a duel with pistols like Hamilton did with Burr in 1804. It doesn't mean clubbing each other on the head with baseball bats just like so-called cavemen were alleged to have done. Today, we have legal recourse. We can also use the law to identify the typical triggers that lead to conflict. And in identifying them, we can do everything within our power to either avoid or resolve them.

Conflict triggers arise from unfairly comparing ourselves with others. They also arise from a lack of fairness, particularly in the workplace. But ask the great Wayne Gretzky and he'll be the first to tell you that they occur on the ice rink as well. Finally, the closer we are to each other, whether in an intimate relationship or along the borders of our properties, the greater the chances of conflict, all of which can still be resolved.

Charles sighed. He decided that John must really be a loser if he chose to bully him on the playground every other day. He had to ask himself: Why can't guys like John pick on guys his own size, and for that matter, mental temperament, and take out their adolescent frustrations on each other, and let other guys-like Charles-quietly get on with their reading, chess games, woodworking or anything else they do to preoccupy themselves with to keep them out of trouble.

It's logical, Charles thought to himself; whenever there's a fight, there's always a loser. Only the thing is, is the guy who's been floored with a bloody nose the real loser on the playground? Inevitably, where there's no right of recourse or no means for someone to legally defend himself, everyone's a loser. The guy on the ground loses because he's hurting. But the bully, still on his two feet, loses as well.

The Pushover

John knows he can get his way with Charles because Charles is what is known as a pushover. But what is a pushover? And how does a pushover handle conflict? Given that John is a bully and wouldn't think twice about using his fists if no one dared to stop him, how would poor Charles handle such a situation?

Given that Charles' intellect is far superior to John's, I'm not entirely sure that he's really a pushover. After all, a pushover is someone who is easily fooled or influenced. Perhaps it would be better to apply that label to John's so-called friends. These are the guys who follow him wherever he goes and will do whatever he tells them to do. Charles, and others who have observed John and his gang from a distance, do, however, wonder if these boys are afraid of John.

Not having a mind of their own, do they simply nod their heads in agreement whenever John makes a remark about something or someone? No doubt, Charles is someone who is ready to hand over his lunch money, and anything else of value, once John demands it from him. But he's not doing so willingly. He's doing so under duress. It's his way of keeping the peace and making sure no further harm comes to him.

Charles' mother cares for him. So does his dad. Having witnessed their time spent in the school principal's office, it's quite possible that they're pushovers as well. After all, they didn't appear to blink an eye when the principal told them that "it is what it is" when they asked what could be done about John's behavior, and how their son could be protected from such bullying. They gave no indication that they disagreed with the principal's philosophy that "boys will be boys."

While we've never encountered her in this observation, John's mother could be a pushover. She's willing to do anything he says. She's willing to give him anything he wants. For that matter, she may find it hard to say no to her husband who, as John's father, might be proud of his exploits. As far as he's concerned, it's been easy to teach his son how to be a real man in the real world.

But in reality, this is not how real men should behave. Moreover, I think the noun "pushover" has been widely misunderstood. Certainly, in the literal sense, a pushover is someone who can be pushed over easily and it might be applied as a strategy during a rules-based football game but in everyday life, this is not how it's implied.

Common Traits of a Pushover, and the Problems They Face

While an original, turn-of-the-century explanation defined a pushover as an easy task to complete, the pushover that we're trying to come to terms with, is faced with several uphill challenges if he persists with his malleable behavior in the workplace. He might think he's being diligent, but he's doing his body and mind no favors when he's the first to arrive at work in the morning, and the last to leave at night.

But whether at work or play, the pushover finds it hard to say no to people. While he continues to seek praise from others, he wrongfully perceives that his performance levels are displeasing to others. That said, he cannot stop apologizing. To most reasonable men, this can be quite irritating. Men with just enough testosterone to mythically move a mountain, also find it ingratiating when the proverbial pushover is unable to or reluctant to speak his mind on any subject under the sun.

Considering the above traits, perhaps poor Charles is a pushover after all. Whether in word or deed, ideally without using his fists, he doesn't ever appear to want to stand up to an adolescent like John. If standing up to a bully was too much for the poor boy, wouldn't it have been better to just run away? As fast as possible?

Running Away from a Damaged Reputation

I wouldn't think any less of Charles if he decided to run away from John. Like the Bob I introduced to you in the previous chapter, I wouldn't go as far as branding Charles a coward either. But would others? Would you? The reality is that no matter who is to blame in the Charles vs. John scenario (is John really to blame?), people, and men in particular, are not as forgiving as I am (and no, I'm *not* a pushover either!).

Charles needs every bit of help he can get. If he never gets to go to college because of poor academic results (always possible for a guy like Charles who is not under pressure to perform), I shudder to think how he might cope during a 12-hour shift at a takeout or sit-down dinner. How would he cope with the demands of the customers? Time being money, his supervisor might be reluctant to keep him on if he keeps on mistiming his orders.

We fail to see how Charles would cope with numerous negative comments to his timid posts on his preferred social media account. Or would people simply ignore the poor young man, and move on to other, juicier posts? Then again, I could say to Charles that he's not missing much. After all, there are always good books to read.

Being at the Bottom of the Food Chain Is No Joke

I can just imagine Charles standing in the lunch queue at school. He could be the last in line. He won't have easy pickings either. He'd just have to take what he's given. Even on a good day, that which is given to him could just as easily be taken away from him. Remember, John? Unless John has managed to get himself expelled, he's still at the same school as Charles.

Being at the bottom of the food chain is no joke. And the longer you keep allowing yourself to be "pushed over," the worse it becomes for you, later on in life.

Let's also assume that Charles has made it that far in life. He got into college. He even went to post-grad school and finished his degree with flying colors. As a young man, not yet in his prime, you would have thought that Charles had the world at his feet. But for poor Charles, it's never going to be as easy as that. It's not easy for regular guys who'll all shout out loud every once in a while if ever asked what they think: No one's eating out of our hands either! You see, regular guys, with or without composure, are still willing to put up a fight whenever they're challenged, whereas poor Charles' natural inclination to retreat may well follow him into adulthood unless he's prepared to do what this book suggests to gain his composure.

The Hot Headed

With flying colors, Charles should impress potential interviewers. But by the time he sits down to an interview, he's in no-man's-land again. Lacking composure, he's not able to ace the interview. Come to think of it, I don't think a hot-headed interviewee like Gary would make it very far either. Not only would he be shown the door, but his interviewer, particularly if she's a woman, might be compelled to call security.

Why would Michelle, Gary's interviewer, have to call security? After all, the two of them were in the middle of an interview, not a conflict? Or were they? Could it be that Gary raised his voice to the point that it alarmed his potential employer? His voice was so loud that people outside the office, waiting patiently for their turn to be interviewed, could hear it.

The raised voice of a hot head—in the middle of a conflict or not—is a clear sign that he could be unreasonably argumentative. He's one of those temperamental men who are not prepared to give others a chance to speak. It's no wonder then that Michelle wants to call security. Even if his jaw was clenched tight, so tight that it would need a visor to unclench, his body language suggested that he was ready to come to blows, if necessary. It sent a shudder down Michelle's sweat-soaked spine.

I'd like to see someone like Gary in the ring. How would he cope against guys better prepared for conflict than him, I wonder?

Hot-Headed Problems in Life

A hot-headed person like Gary can look forward to a lot of problems in life. From what we know about hot heads is that rather than avoid conflicts or at least try to resolve them, they seem to thrive on them.

By now, it's pretty obvious that there's not a chance in hell that Gary's going to be hired by Michelle. He doesn't stand much of a chance elsewhere either. Apart from the fact that he's antisocial in the sense that he doesn't get along with other people, and doesn't care much about their wellbeing, he's not one to take orders from anybody, not even from someone who's supposed to be in charge.

And to make matters worse for Gary-lest we need to remind ourselves-Michelle is a woman. No, it's not a reflection of her. It's just that Gary has misogynistic tendencies, and doesn't do well in intimate relationships. If he was married before, he'd have been divorced by now. For a woman living under the same roof as Gary, it's not safe either. At any moment, he could snap. And when he snaps, he might be inclined to let her have it, in word and deed.

Only in Gary's case, the deed might translate into violence. Fortunately for society at large, the law is against men like Gary. But how unfortunate for Gary if he should ever be arrested. Apart from incarcerating him to teach him a lesson, can someone like Gary be helped? Of course he can. But will he listen?

Fight-or-Flight and Emotional Issues

Men like Gary usually need to undergo therapy to be healed of their wounds. Whether from childhood or due to a recent event in their lives, the therapist would usually have to navigate a few underlying emotional issues that plague hot-headed men. Just because men like Gary want or need to be in control doesn't mean that they're in control. It's usually the other way around. They are insecure to the core. And yes, they're out of control. For far too long, they've become accustomed to fighting and getting their own way. It's always hard for them to learn how or when to back down.

On the verge of a conflict or sensing that a conflict might be imminent, someone like Gary might be prone to what is known as the fight-or-flight response. It happens to the best of us because the fight-or-flight response is a completely natural, human reaction in response to a perceived attack or threat to survival. Come to think of it, Gary might have done well all those thousands of years ago, living in a cave and hunting creatures twice, three times his size.

Someday, I'd like to put Gary in the ring with Marcus. Almost twice the size, and twice the strength of Marcus, you might be inclined to put your money on Gary winning the bout. But the thing is, Marcus has something that Gary's lacking: inner strength. And that, among other traits, is what makes Marcus a champion when it comes to dealing with conflict.

The Champion

When he perceives that he could be in trouble or in danger, the champion doesn't run away. He doesn't run charging into the perceived danger zone like a raging bull either. He first tries to assess what the danger is, if there's even danger at all. If there is, he'll proceed with using instinct to confront the situation. His first priority is to make sure that he's safe. If others are under his care, his priority shifts to them.

A true champion is brave but I doubt very much that he'll put his life on the line without thinking. Rather, if there is a perceived danger, he'll first assess the situation, perhaps even, think twice before reacting to the perceived danger. If the danger is beyond him to manage, he might be inclined to engage a third party. But should he be able to respond to the danger, with full composure as his line of defense, he'll do so within the confines of the laws that govern composure. Or a man in full control of his faculties.

A Champion in Conflict

A true champion is a law-abiding citizen. In the heat of an argument with his spouse or partner, he won't raise his voice or come to blows, in the way that a hothead like Gary might do. Even so, both he and his partner will have done everything in their power to avoid enduring such confrontations in the first place. After all, the first line of defense is always that prevention is better than cure.

Whether a member of Wayne Gretzky's ice hockey team or a workplace leader in his own right, a champion does his level best to make himself aware of any looming tensions. If need be, he might have no alternative but to resort to whistle-blowing tactics if the behavior of others, particularly those who are in positions of responsibility over others. That, in itself, might be an act of bravery. After all, he could be placing himself in the firing line.

How a Champion Resolves Conflict

Even so, he knows his rights. He will also have taken time and trouble to get to know the team well, just like Gretzky would have done. This applies to the workplace as well, and as a manager or supervisor, the champion needs to be clear about the expectations of team conduct. Indeed, not a leader per se, but an effective cog in the engine that turns the wheel of a successful organization, he is a team player and will do everything in his power to stay out of trouble.

This does not mean, however, that he'll be hiding away in an effort to avoid conflict at every turn. After all, the reality is that conflict is always possible wherever there's pressure and an expectation to perform beyond the call of duty. If that's the case, a member of a champion team will act with self-belief, discipline, and confidence.

Common Traits of a Champion

There are other traits to look forward to in a champion. We've already established that he has the courage to act and perform whenever and however necessary. He has goals, he knows how to set them, and going forward, he will certainly be scoring them. But if it's in the greater interests of the team, and there's a better tactical chance that another member of the team will score the goal, he'll make it possible for that player to do so instead.

He is able to do this because he's well aware of the team's tactics. A champion team doesn't resort to cheating to get ahead, it plays by the rules. It can get by with the rules of the game because, like Gretzky during his playing days, it has studied them and strategized around them. The champion has practiced hard as well. But he hasn't allowed his passion and enthusiasm for the game to push himself to the point of injuring himself, causing harm to others, and even suffering a complete burnout.

Success in Conflict Leads to a Better Quality of Life

The champion's attitude to life is always positive. If there is a conflict that needs to be resolved, rather than confronted, he always believes that there will be a positive outcome. A positive attitude also makes it possible to achieve goals. Resilience ensures that problems will be resolved and goals will be achieved afterward.

A champion with a positive attitude toward life and workplace outcomes can only command respect from others. At the same time, respect is always earned. Long after the champion has retired and effectively removed himself from the conflict zone, he continues to enjoy a better quality of life. His discipline and motivation to make financial savings and material gains have allowed for this.

But as he ages as a pillar of wisdom, he'll continue looking after himself. If he has family responsibilities, he'll continue looking after those who still look up to him for advice, support, and even protection.

How to Maintain Composure in a Conflict

How does the true champion of life as we've come to get to know, manage to keep himself together in times of conflict? Not that he's always expecting conflict at every turn, but it could be that he's also prepared himself well ahead of the event. In doing so, he has, more than likely, observed the following rules:

- The champion is aware of his emotions and the impact they might have on others. If confronted by Gary, the hotheaded guy we spoke about earlier, a champion like

Marcus will have assessed his antagonist's temperament before responding to a full-fledged rebuke or confrontation.

- He always strives to see where the other person is coming from. Marcus will want to know why someone like Gary acts out in the way he does. When responding to Gary's outbursts, he might even want to help the guy.

- Doing so, he listens carefully to what the other person is trying to say. Apart from listening to Gary's angry or condescending remarks, someone like Marcus, our resident champion, might even go as far as listening to the advice of others on how to respond to Gary.

- In the event that a conflict does arise, he's focused on his breathing, keeps his emotions in check, keeps his perspective, and doesn't walk away from the conflict. Marcus, the true champion, will stand his ground until the challenge is resolved. He's not being stubborn, he just wants to see a peaceful end to the conflict. Calm, and in control of his emotions, he has the confidence to stay the course, rather than retreat or give in, as someone like Charles, the pushover, might have done.

Winning the Mental Battle

In the event that he is called upon to do battle—figuratively speaking—in a conflict, the true champion is already halfway there in terms of winning the mental battle. While he might be required to withhold what he's thinking and feeling at any given moment, he's not attempting to play mind games in order to intimidate his opponent. That, however, is usually permissible during a sporting contest, in which a spirit of goodwill prevails in terms of the rules of the game being played.

If there is a winner, the loser must lose well. A sporting gesture acknowledges the loss with a playful warning that he will do better next time. The loser must also learn how to manage his own internal conflict before taking up another challenge. He can do that by observing the following steps:

- Identify and acknowledge his conflict.

- Explore the trigger of his conflict.

- Calm down his mind before trying to find a solution to his internal conflict.

To calm his mind, the conflict-ridden man must determine what's needed for him to feel safe before making his decision. He needs to trust himself and his inner wisdom, and not worry about what others may think or say about the decision he's about to make.

The perennial defeatist needs to face his fears. He also needs to address his lack of self-esteem. Sooner rather than later, he must accept the consequences such a lack of self-esteem has in different areas of his life. Not for a moment longer must he allow himself to be regarded as a pushover by others, whether his wife, kids, colleagues, or next-door neighbor.

Here's an opportunity for you to self-reflect and look at those areas of your life where you've been lacking, whether in the home, the workplace, and the way you manage your finances. Your lack of self-esteem, which could have been caused by previous traumatic experiences in your life, causes you to lack the confidence you need to compose yourself to right the wrongs in your life, whether through circumstances not of your making or through your own lack of will.

Finally, you can make use of the following steps to begin the process of elevating your low self-esteem:

- Forget for a moment your worst qualities and write a list of the things you most admire about yourself.

- Step outside your comfort zone, and stop trying to please everyone at the same time by thinking of yourself for a change. Think about what makes you happy.

- Think about your uniqueness and stop comparing yourself to others.

- Forgive yourself for past transgressions or mistakes, move past negative people by setting up boundaries for yourself, and move on with your life.

Believe in Yourself

Believe in yourself. Believe that you have what it takes to succeed in life. In your struggle against adversity, with or without everyday conflict, believe that you can overcome anything or anyone that stands in your way. There's no need for you to overwhelm yourself with drastic changes to your life, and the way that you live it when you can simply make small changes that will make all the difference in the world.

Even the smallest, positive changes you make to how you perceive everyday life events, can help you deal with any confrontation before it balloons into a great confrontation. Believing in yourself means that you have confidence in your abilities. Tackle the challenges of life like a gentleman so that others may respect you for trying. Have no fear of failure, even when mistakes are made. After all, if your mindset is positive, you can learn from your mistakes.

Benefits to Look Forward To

Persistently delaying the inevitable is perhaps one of the greatest mistakes a pushover can make. The more he procrastinates, the worse things become for him. And while the poor pushover continues to wallow in the consequences of his delays, always running away from confrontation, turning left and right to find a suitable hiding place where none is to be found, the true champion continues to reap the benefits of his full composure, particularly in the face of conflict. Make a mental note of the following benefits the champion is enjoying:

- On the brink of a conflict, the champion is able to manage his stress levels quickly, while remaining alert and calm.

- The champion is in control of his emotions and behavior.

- He can pay attention to the feelings of others, as well as his own.

- He is always aware of differences and is always able to respect them.

- While making himself fully aware of the needs of others, he is always able to effectively communicate his needs to them.

If you can overcome your fear of asking questions about your own behavior, and ask the true champion what must be done to deal with, and overcome a conflict without losing your cool, I'm certain that he'll be more than happy to share with you what he's learned and experienced. It's not as though he's about to give away trade secrets. As far as he is concerned, all that is needed is to observe the basics of keeping your composure while managing and resolving a conflict.

Resolving Conflict Calmly

His ability to indulge in a sense of humor without offending helps the true champion to resolve conflict calmly. Indeed, he's even able to instill a sense of calm in others. When he's around, there's never a need for angry outbursts, and certainly no need to resort to fisticuffs in a way only a bully knows how.

Let me elaborate on the above benefits that the champion could share with you. If you follow the champion's example, you'll not only listen to what is being said at the moment, but you'll be listening for meaning as well. Active listening skills not only help you to make a connection with others, they help you to connect more deeply to your own needs and emotions. Always bear in mind that your ability to listen to others strengthens, informs, and makes it easier for them to hear what you've got to say (Robinson et al., 2024).

Also, there's no sense in trying to win an argument that you could lose. Rather, make conflict resolution your priority. In doing so, you remain respectful of the other person, as well as his point of view.

When you're in the middle of a conflict, there's no sense in casting your mind elsewhere. It doesn't help if you lose eye contact with the person who is perceptively opposing you. Doing so means that you've probably lost his respect. That said, focus only on the present, and hold no grudges about what may have happened in the past. If this is something that still preoccupies you, learn to let go. In the event that no agreement is possible, prepare to "agree to disagree." Rest easy in the knowledge that this stalemate is not a reflection of your effort to resolve a conflict.

Half the battle may already have been won—if indeed it is a battle—if you're willing to forgive. No matter who is right or wrong in the conflict, bear in mind that the negative preoccupation of wanting to punish your opponent will only cause you more stress. And by looking forward to the long-term results of conflict resolution, you're not bypassing the conflict you're in.

The harsh reality, if it can be termed that, is that you also need to be aware of your weaknesses. But by making yourself aware, you're not ignoring your strengths either. Knowing both your strengths and weaknesses also allows you to "pick your battles." If a looming conflict appears to be beyond you to resolve, attempt to seek help from those who are better positioned to manage the conflict, and attempt to find a resolution. Doing this does not mean that you're running away from the conflict.

In the meantime, you can still learn to be assertive and set your boundaries without causing offense.

How to Be More Assertive Without Causing Offense

I like to keep the peace, no matter where I am, and no matter who I'm engaging with. And like you, I hate conflict. But as young Charles found, to his dismay, there's nothing to be gained from running away from a conflict. There's nothing to be gained from suffering in silence either. And like Charles, perhaps you'd like to be able to speak up without causing your perceived opponent to be offended by what you've said. More than likely, he's quite familiar with the use of the "I" statement. After all, he uses it often enough himself, doesn't he?

By using the "I" statement more often than you're used to, you're able to let others know what you're thinking or feeling without pointing fingers. You're not blaming others for your predicament. You're simply voicing your opinion, as is your right. It is far better than remaining silent. But if this new form of assertiveness still scares you, there's nothing stopping you from practicing what you want to say. Whether you do this in front of a mirror or with someone you trust or value (and ideally, it will be the latter), is entirely up to you, just as long as you practice.

Come to think of it, practicing in front of a mirror is not a bad idea at all. After all, you can then check your body language, as well as your facial expressions. In this scenario, you want to be devoid of anger or frustration. You want to be the epitome of calm, always able to keep your emotions in check. While practicing your use of the "I" statement, you can also practice your use of the "no" statement. You can, and must, learn to say no, with or without conflict.

What I like about saying no is that there's no need for you to explain yourself. It's a sentence all on its own. If you believe in yourself, you believe in what you're saying or doing. I have found that no matter what you may think others might be saying about you behind your back or internally, this direct approach can work miracles. It can at least get others to stop what they're doing and pay attention to what you might be going through. Always remember that rarely does the so-called silent treatment work. It only burns with resentment and could cause further misunderstanding.

How to Establish Your Boundaries

But when you say "no" or "I" don't fold your arms or legs. If you do that, you're giving yourself away. Also, you exude confidence and sincerity when you're able to maintain eye contact. Your facial expression can be neutral but I believe it could be even more effective if you're able to maintain a positive expression throughout. This is also a great way of showing others that you're calm. But if this is something you still need to work on, breath slowly, while keeping your voice even and firm. Again, any trace of nervousness in your voice or body language could be giving the game away.

In the meantime, if you're able to establish your boundaries without batting an eyelid, you'll be able to build relationships and assume responsibility for your needs without fear. When you place your stake in the ground, there's no need for you to feel guilty either. But in order to ensure that no one gets hurt or offended by what you say, make sure that you've gathered enough information about your circumstances and are able to list your most important priorities. Be consistent when stating your case. Attempt to shift the goalposts too often in an effort to compromise, and you might be giving the game away. Again.

Remember that it's okay to brace yourself for some conflict in the form of rebuttals or objections. But by that time, you've done your work, just as long as you haven't made the conflict a personal one. If you respect yourself, you'll respect the views or feelings of others, particularly if they too are practicing what you're attempting here, always bearing in mind that respect is earned. In this case, others will learn to respect you by the actions you take. They'll learn to respect the boundaries you've set for yourself. And they'll respect you for making this much about yourself known to them.

At the best of times in family situations, my dad relied on projecting himself as the "strong and silent" one, particularly when these situations were stressful. It remains to be seen whether he was successful in this. After all, I cannot speak for others (my mom, and two brothers), and only vouch for the one-on-one interactions I've had with my dad. But I'm led to believe that my dad's ability to resolve conflict in the workplace, if and when it occurred, was mostly successful. Years of experience also provided him with the leadership skills to manage teams and help his company realize its objectives.

We'll be talking about leadership in this book's penultimate chapter. In the meantime, let's look at the strategies required for finding common ground with a view to achieving solutions.

Finding Common Ground That Is Solutions-Based

Over the years, I've learned a lot from my dad's example since leaving the family home. Apart from learning to stand on my own two feet, I've learned that striving to find common ground with others who may seek to differ from me doesn't compromise me nor does it weaken me. It certainly doesn't weaken my resolve to remain fully composed in every area of my life, always aware that through no fault of my own, conflict could arise at any moment. At the same time, I've learned to man up.

By "manning up," I'm not attempting to assert myself over women or men that are perceived to be weaker than me. Rather, I'm showing others-perceptively stronger than me-that I'm greater than the sum of my parts. I don't say this in a prideful way. Rather, I'm asserting my need to be responsible and live up to my obligations. I'm also game for a challenge but continue to learn to not accept challenges that are way beyond me at this stage of my life.

Working on my need to remain an active listener remains a full-time job, as it should be for you as well. It can be easy to talk about the things you're most passionate about, and not give others a chance to speak, particularly if the subject doesn't interest you much. That said, I particularly enjoy sharing common interests and values, and I relish the opportunity to seek these in the heat of a conflict. I can do this because I am able to hold my own in terms of what I believe and value in life. I'm also up to the task of generating alternatives but must acknowledge that this can take time. It also requires patience to evaluate a list of mutual desires before agreeing to a strategy that can help us meet them.

Let me close this chapter with an example of how we should negotiate with composure, and without losing our cool if the negotiation is required to extricate ourselves from a potential conflict.

Cool Negotiation Tactics

The cool negotiator is able to use his best powers of persuasion, confident in the knowledge that he's not out to gain the upper hand in a potential conflict. Rather, his open and positive mind has allowed him to gauge a diverse variety of interests and concerns that could potentially lead to a solution. The cool negotiator is not seeking to curry favor to help serve his own selfish interests (he has interests but they are not selfish). Rather, he is seeking to build rapport or support for the realization of goals that please and help every party in the negotiations.

The cool negotiator won't be acting alone. If he's in a leadership position, he's utilized the skills of his team to research a list of what they conclude may be the best conflict resolution going forward. He trusts his team and has a hand in giving them the responsibility to come up with the best solutions. Finally, the team enjoys longevity. There is rarely a desire to move elsewhere. After all, what joy is there in leaving a winning team?

Whether the cool negotiator is compelled to make a presentation on his own or is able to assemble his team for the gathering, they are all able to handle the pressure. Pressure is not something you're able to get away with. But you can learn to deal with it with composure. This is something you'll do in the next chapter.

6. Handling High-Stake Environments with Composure

A man in full. More to the point: A man with his hands full. This is a man who loves to take on the jobs that others loathe or fear. He seems to thrive under pressure. Everyone around him loves him. His extra pound of flesh is taking a lot of weight off their shoulders. Eager to please others, particularly his superiors, this young man is no pushover, let me tell you. As far as he's concerned, let others think what they will of him. He has plans. He's ambitious and believes that by making the sacrifices he's making today-spending extra hours at his desk, putting himself through grad school at his own cost, and not giving in to weekend temptations, he's going to reap the benefits later.

The man with his hands full is still young. He's got plenty to prove. Not so much to all those around him, certainly not his superiors but to himself. He continues to test unchartered territory, pushing himself just that much harder to see if he can withstand the pressure. On the surface, it doesn't appear so. As far as others are concerned, this man is certifiable. He's a glutton for punishment. But he's got a soul. He's got a pragmatic soul which says that learning to deal with pressures at such an early stage of his life will only serve his best interests later on in life. As far as he is concerned, it is all good practice for the future which his dad likes to tell him will only get harder.

But as far as I'm concerned, this young man needs to slow down.

I'm not discouraging him from going the extra mile. It's just that I'd like him to pace himself better. I fail to see that this young man is being pragmatic about the way he goes about his work/life balance. As far as I'm concerned, he could be an old man by the time he reaches the age of 30.

In the meantime, you might have noticed my use of the "I" statement. Indeed, in this scenario, I am voicing my objection. I am also curious. I'd like to know: just how does he do it? And if he makes it to 30 in one piece, will he be ready, willing, and able to face the pressures of life that most men wouldn't mind trading for a life of ease under the palm trees, down by the beach?

The Bottle Job

Maybe Bert the Boss was a nice guy for a while. After all, he gave Jack one stay of execution after another. For a long time, Jack got away with firing offenses. One of the things that caused a lot of distress among his co-workers was his drinking habit. No, it wasn't the occasional Friday lunchtime beer that could be excused after a hard work week; it was heavy drinking.

They never saw him drink on the job. They just knew he had a drinking problem. They could smell it on his breath. And it was during their lighter moments that they even went as far as name-calling Jack, the Bottle Job. But interestingly enough, there's an underlying meaning to this label. Let's explore it.

Great footballers they may have been in their day but French legends Zinedine Zidane and Eric Cantona are what the English football fans like to refer to as a bottle job. It has nothing to do with their off-the-pitch drinking habits. It has everything to do with their spectacular and respective collapses under pressure.

Even so, I still wonder if the bottle job acronym is apt for these two great players. After all, their spectacular on-the-pitch clashes were surely isolated moments of madness during long, illustrious playing careers.

Back at the gym, we of course, knew little of "bottle jobs." Our concerns were about what happened in the ring. We were also concerned about protecting the head from potential blows that could cause concussion, and even worse injuries. But in doing the research of this (originally) British term, we couldn't help being amazed at the definitions that were thrown at us, with water bottle inspector and water boy being the most common "job titles."

But in order to fully appreciate the English football analogy, it might be useful to use it as a metaphor for real-life situations. That said, a bottle job may do well for a reasonable amount of time but ultimately caves into pressure. He could resort to drinking or other unsavory habits in a vain attempt to deal with the pressure. But if he's a well-behaved chap, he picks himself up and tries to shoot straight again.

But only to fall into the gutter again.

So, pity the poor bottle job then. He has so many frustrations. To others, he's an abject failure. Miserable as hell, he believes he's a failure as well. As far as he's concerned, he might as well give up: there's not much chance of him ever recovering, and making something of himself. He's also suffered so much reputational damage, surely there's no one left to give him another chance.

Actually, there is. What do you think? Do you think we should give the bottle job another shot? Do you believe he deserves a chance? Having come close to being an abject failure in life yourself, you might be inclined to agree that, yes, the bottle job deserves a second chance in life, as do we all.

The Cool Hand

Knowing that I was a lover of movies, particularly ones that featured everyone's favorite action heroes, I've lost count of how many times I've been asked: Andrew, what do you make of James Bond? Is he awesome or what? Indeed, unlike Rocky Balboa in the ring, the suave secret agent takes on villains twice his size and status dressed in an evening suit, bowtie, and all. It must take a heck of a lot of composure to raise a stunt like that.

But like today's beauty queens, fans value their heroes more for their intellect. It's more about brains than braun, and it's no less the case for James Bond who's had to endure no less than half-a-dozen reincarnations. I remain awe-struck at the way Bond was able to swindle his way through Le Chiffre's intimidating mind games at the poker table in one of the best Bond movies I've seen, *Casino Royale*.

The ladies' man never raises a sweat, always performing well under pressure under any circumstances. Not even Daniel Craig's interpretation of a dirt-stained and bruised Bond, broken nose and all, can disguise the fact that "Bond, James Bond," will remain fully composed for at least the next six incarnations of his character. Even though he always appears to be looking for trouble, always out to prove himself, his character will never be assassinated.

Never mind his uncanny ability to charm every woman he lays his eyes on (with great eye contact) but have you noticed how well James Bond dresses, even when casually? To my mind, this is the visual epitome of a fully composed man. He's not necessarily vain but does take pride in his appearance. Of course, it goes without saying that he's far better dressed than the average man who cares for nothing more than being comfortable. Or so he alleges.

With a stomach bulge he ought to be ashamed of (he probably is), it's not easy for the average man to dress as smoothly as James Bond does. The average Joe doesn't have muscles either like GI Joe does. He doesn't work out much, going no further than the weekend biceps curls with beer cans in hand. Standing around the barbecue fire, the average, working men still ask each other: Just how does he do it? How does James Bond always get the girl, and how come we can't?

Nonplussed, they can only stare at each other's bellies, and nod their heads in shame.

Just because James Bond does it, doesn't mean that you have to do it too: always looking for trouble, and trying to prove yourself. Looking for trouble just happens to be Bond's full-time job, in more ways than one. It's yours too if you just happen to be a law enforcement officer. But as a mentally composed man, dedicated to upholding the law, you'll be striving to help others keep out of trouble as well.

In real life, the well-composed man has accepted the inevitability of there being trouble down the line. But in doing so, he has also prepared himself well to deal with it. It is not as if he craves pressure, perhaps his body language suggests otherwise sometimes, it's just that he's acclimated himself well to dealing with pressure. Moreover, he's going to strive to make every sense out of every growth opportunity he's been given to learn how to become stronger in adversity.

Let's be honest, no one, not even the toughest guys, likes pressure, least of all me. But we've all come to terms with it and accepted it as a daily fact of life. And if you haven't done so by now, I'd recommend that you don't put this off any longer than you have to, and start to learn how to deal with pressure. Rest assured that for the duration of this chapter, I'll show you how this is done.

How to Perform Under Pressure

The ability to perform under pressure differs from person to person. Due to our upbringing and our unique set of values and beliefs, we all perceive and deal with pressure in different ways. The parish priest may choose to forgive (but won't forget) while the judge is obligated to reprimand. While the priest leaves it up to God to forgive the transgressor, the judge delegates the responsibility of determining whether an offender is guilty or not to a jury, selected at random but seated as representatives of broader society nonetheless.

Such people have a moral obligation to compose themselves well in the eyes of others. After all, others are looking up to them for leadership and guidance. The preparation that LeBron James puts into a basketball match is hardly the same that Tyson Fury would need to put in to reclaim his title as the undisputed champion of the world. Their mental preparation, however, is on a par with the pressures they're usually faced with. It's not only the pressure on the court or in the ring but the expectations of millions of fans from around the globe watching their every move.

Preparation

Let's assume that Charles, the troubled young student I introduced to you in the previous chapter, has made amends. He is now at college and is preparing for his first end-of-year exams. Ultimately, he passes with flying colors. Apart from the early preparation he put into his lessons during the first semester, he already enjoyed an advantage that fellow students didn't appear to share: His love for reading.

If other students had followed his example during their high school years, they would also have learned to read for meaning. But no matter how well you prepare for your exams, you would still have to prepare yourself mentally, and practice self-care. Today's great sportsmen and women, from Lebron James to US tennis star Coco Gauff, are all familiar with the practice, which essentially includes regular training, along with the exercise habits required to sustain them in practice and in sport.

Eating habits would have to be healthy, and as Arnold Schwarzenegger has stressed in numerous motivational talks, these sportsmen and women's sleep environments would have to be sublime. Portuguese superstar, Cristiano Ronaldo is another fine example who, quite literally, stands head and shoulders above the rest.

Importance of Good Preparation

Ronaldo's longevity reminds me of the poor example set by another Manchester United great, George Best. He was well and truly gifted but ultimately, due to his poor lifestyle habits, including alcohol abuse, he couldn't sustain himself. In his heyday, he may have had composure on the field but in life after football, he was sorely lacking this important ingredient required to live and perform under pressure.

The importance of good preparation cannot be emphasized more. Good preparation before an important event in your life provides you with the breathing space to relax. In the event, it allows you to do your best. Thanks to your good preparation before the event, you are confident and composed, knowing full well that you are going to succeed in realizing the objectives you set for yourself prior to the big event, whether an end-of-year exam, college basketball play-off match, or career-defining interview.

As a fully composed young man, you are confident but not complacent the night before an important exam. Fully aware of your limitations as a student working under pressure, you've also practiced good time management throughout your academic year. You have also practiced well in mock exam scenarios, not only absorbing the content of your material but training your mind to pace yourself with composure throughout your sitting, usually lasting anything from one to three hours, depending on the level of your studies.

How to Better Prepare Yourself

Like Charles, train yourself to read as often as possible. This suggestion assumes that you need to mentally prepare yourself for an exam. At the same time, allow yourself to take a break. You can do this if you've practiced good time management. There's no need to stress about falling behind with your schedule because good preparation requires you to make plans ahead of time.

Like Charles, this is something you can do at the beginning of your semester but if you're already halfway through the year, you can still make plans. Say to yourself that there's no better day than today to start fresh. Planning requires you to ask questions of yourself. Do this as honestly as possible. At the same time, there's no need for you to overwhelm yourself with worry about what seems impossible to you if you focus on what you know. Working on what you know will allow you to move closer toward overcoming what previously seemed unknown to you.

No doubt, changes may need to be made to how you spend your time. But when you embrace these changes, think in terms of change being as good as a holiday. There is nothing better. So, keeping that good news in mind, ask yourself this question: Are you doing all that you can to prepare yourself for future events or challenges?

Why Practice Makes Perfect

Without putting any pressure on yourself, practice deliberately. If you need to change the way you're doing things, always remember that anything new that you're attempting will get better as long as you keep practicing. What you achieve midway through your new schedule, doesn't have to be perfect. It will be perfect or as close to perfect as you can make it by the time you've reached the end of your challenge. In any event, through regular practice, you're already increasing the odds of being successful at a time when it should matter.

While old habits continue to be hard to break, breaking them will become easier, just as long as you keep on practicing. Through regular practice, you are already in a developmental stage of replacing habits that may have impeded your ability to act under pressure. Always remember that the more you practice new ways of doing things, particularly when under pressure, the better you'll become at absolving yourself of the pressure you're feeling.

Preparing for Unexpected Outcomes

Inevitably, more pressure is shifted onto your shoulders when unexpected events, not previously expected or planned for, occur. Today, there's no need for you to stress any further because it's also possible for you to prepare for unexpected outcomes. Here's how it's done.

Simply put, without ignoring your regular planning routine, prepare yourself for what can be termed contingency planning. In this test case scenario, there are four important steps to bear in mind. But before I present you with these steps, make a note of what contingency planning entails. In business, companies utilize a risk management strategy which helps them to foresee potential disruptions to their business. Contingency planning helps you to minimize disruption. It is what is commonly referred to as your plan B.

With contingency planning, you might not be able to mitigate the unexpected event altogether but can develop the problem-solving skills required to deal with it. We'll talk more about problem-solving in the next chapter. In the meantime, the following steps will help you to deal with the challenge of an unexpected event:

- Identify the triggers that could lead up to this unexpected event.

- Using a hypothetical scenario, examine the events that could unfold.

- Alert all those within your immediate circle. You might need to enlist their help to overcome the challenge you're faced with.

- Practice the worst-case scenario as you anticipate it may happen.

Warming-Up for the Big Event

Charles, previously known as a pushover but from this day forward, known as a champion in the making, is preparing for his big day. He has already graduated from college. His excellent results allowed him to gain what could be a career-defining interview at a major publishing company. Not yet able to rid himself of his nervous habits, he's prepared a contingency plan that serves as his warm-up on the morning of his interview. With the plan in front of him, Charles reminds himself to do the following:

- Focus on being as relaxed and composed as possible. Not more than an hour before the exam, and even moments before the exam has commenced, Charles will have done a couple of breathing exercises to ensure this.

- Talk positively to yourself, always reminding yourself that you're going to do well. This task becomes easier for you the more you've prepared yourself well by following a manageable schedule.

- Practice deep breathing by focusing on your breath to help relax both your mind and body.

- Remember to exercise regularly because this will help you to feel energized before the event. Ensure that whatever exercise you're doing is not too strenuous. Remember that you also need to sleep well the night before an exam.

- Go through your talking points to help you visualize and memorize responses to questions your interviewer could ask you.

Charles has also negotiated the public transport timetable rather well, allowing himself an hour or so at a nearby coffee shop to enjoy his favorite latte. He is relaxed, and there's no need to rush to the fourth floor in the building where the publishing company's offices are located.

I'm Excited, Aren't You?

There's one thing Charles can't help while he waits in the reception area to be called in for his interview. Previously, he would also be nervous as hell. But today, all he is going through is a sense of nervous excitement. He knows that he still needs to compose himself. So, when we're feeling excited about an upcoming event that could yield positive results, what do we do to compose ourselves?

Again, it's necessary to mentally prepare yourself before the event. In terms of composing yourself to alleviate the excitement you might be feeling, bear the following strategies in mind:

- Familiarize yourself with the event, and learn everything you can about what may happen.

- Continue making use of the above warm-up plan that Charles has used.

- Avoid fantasizing about what might happen and don't raise your expectations.

- Dismiss the significance of the desired outcomes. But don't dismiss the possibility of failure.

- Distance yourself from the event.

Performance

I don't anticipate a lack of performance when I deliver my manuscript to the publisher. At the same time, I'm realistic enough to accept that I still need to prepare myself. I need to make sure that the delivery of my performance meets the expectations of my publisher. Even so, I'd still like to visualize exceeding all expectations. Have I raised the bar too high? Am I getting ahead of myself? Or am I being positive and ambitious, fully believing that there is always a silver lining to overcoming any or all high-pressure events in my life?

In this section, we're going to address our performance capabilities by making sure that we remain composed. At the same time, we need to remind ourselves that if all else fails, there is still a plan B to look forward to.

Coping Mechanisms to Help You Regain Your Composure

In order to help you keep calm in tense situations, I'd like you to focus on your breathing. In a later section, I'll provide you with a breathing exercise. In the meantime, make a note in your journal that you could use the short breathing exercise as a form of mindfulness meditation. It allows you to focus on the present moment, drawing attention to how your physical senses react to tense situations.

The breathing exercise is also good preparation for you to dig a little deeper into your emotional side to find positive emotions that help you to cope. The breathing exercise also helps you to stay calm. If you're physically active, doing some sport in your free time, you can also practice what is known as progressive muscle relaxation before and after your exercise session or sporting event.

Progressive muscle relaxation requires you to tense your muscles before relaxing them again. It is a great technique to help you to reduce the stress and anxiety you feel in your body.

Why It's Necessary to Slow Down

Along with cognitive behavioral therapy (CBT) or dialectical behavior therapy (DBT), which he could introduce to you to help you cope with the pressure you're feeling, your therapist—if you feel a need to see one—will more than likely encourage you to slow down. Here's why this is necessary. The first thing your therapist might say to you is that slowing down is essential for your personal growth. And the rest that you give yourself, is a lot more helpful than you might think.

Moreover, when you allow yourself to slow down, you're creating space in which you can reflect on your thoughts, emotions, and whatever it is that you're going through. Slowing down helps you to gain a better understanding of yourself as a man. It also gives you space to reflect on your ambitions. Slowing down helps you to focus on areas of your personal development that might need improvement. It gives you the opportunity to make conscious choices that also align with your true desires.

It goes without saying that at present, your deepest desire might be to get yourself out of the mess you're in. As you think about this, be still. Think about the practical, self-care tasks that you would need to accomplish to prepare your body and mind to cope better with what you're going through.

Use Grounding Techniques

Being a composed man, you could feel that you've done well in keeping yourself grounded in the figurative sense. But lacking composure (remind yourself that you're still a work in progress), you can introduce grounding techniques—in the literal sense—to your mindfulness and self-care practices. Moreover, slowing down and the ability to breathe more easily are both grounding exercises.

Grounding exercises' main purpose is to help you relax when you're under pressure. It is a time for personal reflection, something that you can do at any time of the day, and in any place that provides the ambiance for perfect reflection. For instance, a walk in the park at a quiet time of the day is far better than navigating a busy mall during peak hours.

It's no secret that I love my walking time but I also use the gym to ground myself. Like the well-composed chap I introduced you to earlier, I'll do a round of stretching exercises before I commence any form of a serious workout. I'm mostly alone in the gym at this time of the weekend, so it does me no harm to put on some of my favorite jazz numbers over the speakers.

Then again, and if I'm honest with you, I'd have to say that listening to jazz while I'm reading in the early morning or evening is my favorite downtime.

Focus On Your Breathing

To help keep yourself calm and composed when you're faced with work/life pressure, I'd like you to focus on your breathing. A breathing exercise can be practiced regularly whenever you're feeling the pressure to succeed or overcome. It is particularly useful when the pressure's been mounting, and it's about to reach boiling point, and I dare say that the breathing exercise—it doesn't need to take longer than five minutes to complete-could be particularly useful for someone like Gary (you'll remember him as the hot head from the previous chapter).

Apart from alleviating stress, this breathing exercise is also designed to improve your lungs' capacity to function. It improves the oxygen and carbon dioxide exchange, and I believe it's a great exercise for guys who are still trying to quit smoking. Easy to do, the pursed-lips breathing technique requires you to observe the following steps:

- Mouth closed, inhale slowly through your nostrils.

- Purse your lips as if you're about to blow on something.

- Then breathe out as slowly as possible through those pursed lips. Breathing out should take twice as long as it took for you to breathe in.

- If you feel as though you could do with another round, repeat the steps.

Physical Displays of Composure

Whether you're dealing with a conflict, communicating with a difficult customer, advocating for change in a discriminatory environment, or dealing with life-affirming challenges, it's also important that you show others that you're composed. You need to show others that you're in control of the situation. You need to show others who wouldn't mind seeing the end of you that you're not about to lose control of your life. And you need to show those who depend on you that you've got the game in hand. The game may be a difficult one to win but your positivity needs to show that it's possible to win. But if not, you and your team go down fighting with your heads held high.

You need to reassure yourselves that you gave it your best shot and that the best is yet to come. Simply put, there's always room for improvement, no matter how many Champions League or NBA titles you've won. As I recall, the LA Lakers' LeBron James has lost more battles than he's won. And yet still, he's everyone's winner. He's still their champion, and will no doubt be entered into the NBA's Hall of Fame records book, alongside the Boston Celtics' Larry Bird, and the Chicago Bulls' Michael Jordan.

In the previous chapter, I listed the requirements for maintaining your composure, and now see no reason why I shouldn't provide you with a summarized reminder of what it takes to be a champion in conflict. Take the following leadership advice to avoid later feelings of regret, for example:

- Don't let emotions get in your way.

- Don't take things personally.

- Delay your reaction.

- Remain fearless.

- Respond decisively.

- Keep yourself accountable.

- And act like you've been there, and done that before.

Date Night, Not Fright Night

Finally, after months of trying, it's your date night. You and your online partner have finally decided that you like and trust each other enough to meet in person. But because you both have romantic feelings for each other, you need to make the night as special as possible. There's no need to be nervous. I realize that people's impressions of each other change once they've met in person but if you groom yourself emotionally and physically, why should you fail?

Act like a gentleman. Think like a gentleman. Dress like a gentleman. Open doors for the lady and doors will be opened for you. While seated at the dining table, adopt a confident but relaxed posture. This will help the lady to relax. Once she's relaxed, she'll want to talk, and when she does, listen intently, leaning forward slightly, and show her that you're interested in what she's saying, always remembering to maintain eye contact. Finally, it goes without saying that you'll need to be on your best behavior as far as table manners go.

Pressure Makes Diamonds

Indeed, diamonds are a girl's best friend. Or so the song goes. But in the human spirit, what is a diamond? If you're a well-groomed and confident man, you can be a girl's best friend too. There's always something rather special about having a diamond around the house. The man's a rough diamond, of that you can be sure but along with his life partner's influence, there's nothing stopping him from becoming a polished diamond.

Me, on the other hand, prefer the psychological definition of this much-loved gem. In essence, the definition is nothing more than an acronym which refers to eight sociological situations, namely

- Duty

- Intellect

- Adversity

- Mating

- Optimism

- Negativity

- Deception

- Sociability

On that score, neither a pushover nor a hot head can be regarded as a diamond. But a champion can. So too, the captain of your team.

How to Be the Captain of Your Team

Being a sportsman myself, I particularly enjoy the sports analogy applied. I was also particularly thrilled to discover during my research for this chapter what two sports psychologists refer to as the "three C's" of a successful team captain. To my mind, being a successful team captain doesn't imply that you're winning every game you're drawn to play. It does, however, imply that you're leading by example and that you're consistent.

That takes care of one of the C's. What about the other two? The number one quality of a great captain is that he cares for the team he's representing. Treating all his players with equal respect, he's genuinely concerned about their well-being, particularly when they're under pressure, and perhaps even on a losing streak. But if that captain's courageous and leading by example, there's no doubt in my mind that he'll be back next season. There's nothing more that both players and their supporters enjoy than a Captain Courageous who's willing to put his body on the line for the team.

Finally, and in the spirit of the great Wayne Gretzky, and even Siya Kolisi, captain of the four-time and back-to-back world rugby cup-winning champions, South Africa, otherwise known to their foes as the Springboks, a great captain is consistent in giving 100% effort during every practice and game. Caring, courageous, and consistent, it doesn't matter if you're on the bench next Saturday. Remember that you're always going to be a part of the team.

Go the Extra Mile Without Hurting

In the workplace, it is no different. In the next chapter, you're going to read a story about Jack. This is not a spoiler alert but I need to tell you that he was never part of that office's team. Never mind going the extra mile for the sake of the team, this was a guy who consistently refused to show up on time, personal problems notwithstanding. I'd also like to reassure you that by doing more than is asked of you doesn't make you a pushover either.

Rather, you're switched on and you've familiarized yourself with three crucial ingredients that separate you from the so-called losers who may not even move a muscle even if you enticed them with the proverbial carrot stick treatment. You understand your role as a valued member of the team, and how it contributes toward their objectives. Secondly and thirdly, you not only believe in your leadership structures, you also show leadership potential and are not afraid to communicate clearly and openly with the higher-ups.

Finally, if you're not rewarded with improved remuneration or a promotion in your current role, you will be rewarded in the future, just as long as you persevere and stay true to your values and goals.

A Journaling Thought or Two

I'd also like to encourage you once more to start journaling your thoughts on a regular basis. I'd recommend that you start with one journal note a day. That said, there's no requirement for you to compose long essays. There's no need for you to worry about who's going to read it or check it for grammar and typo errors. One of the fundamentals of the journal exercise is that your journal is reserved for your private thoughts. No-one else is going to read what you're thinking, not unless you want them to.

Once you've acclimated yourself to this short exercise after a few days, I recommend that you take your journaling a step further by recording your thoughts at least three times a day. For instance, a noted thought or two can be one of the first things you do before you go to work in the morning. By the time the lunch bell has rung, you can spend a few more moments reflecting on how the day has been for you so far.

Finally, spend a few more moments reflecting on the day at least an hour before you go to bed.

If the day hasn't gone as planned, try not to get too caught up in your emotions. Rather, reflect on what may have gone wrong, and what you could have done to improve your circumstances. Indeed, the next chapter will help you to build momentum because it's going to deal specifically with how we should solve our problems. Under the current circumstances, assuming that the day didn't go well for you, reassure yourself that tomorrow will be a better day.

7. Problem-Solving

Jack is being read the riot act. Just moments ago, and without any prior notice, he was hauled into the boss' office. Of course, Bert the Boss had to wait at least an hour before Jack finally slid behind his desk, like the slippery snake that everyone around him thought he was. It was clear as daylight that no one liked him, and quite frankly, it would not matter to them if he never showed up for work. Ever again. In fact, they were all secretly hoping Bert the Boss was going to show Jack the door.

As far as they were concerned, Jack was not a team player. When jobs needed to be done, he never seemed to move a muscle. He was last in of course, but always first out, and at critical moments of the month when deadlines had to be met, he always seemed to find an excuse for making a quick get-away. So, Bert the Boss had no alternative but to read the riot act to Jack the Loser. We cannot call him a Born Loser because we're convinced that Jack was not always like this.

We wonder what happened to him during the intervening years after he left college. He escaped with mediocre results, and perhaps it is Bert the Boss's fault. After all, he had read the poor guy's dull resume. He surely couldn't have expected much from this sore loser. Short of leadership skills in every sense of the word, Bert the Boss thought he could squeeze just enough effort out of this mediocre little man. And by the time demands for pay raises were being made by all and sundry, Bert the Boss thought he could save the company a bundle by paying Jack, and one or two others just like him, below the belt.

In all the time that I've been at the gym, I've never seen Perry swing a blow below the belt. In boxing, that's not only cheating but could be fatal to the opponent, the wearing of protection guards notwithstanding. I have, however, been watching his performance in the ring a lot lately. You see, Perry's a lot smaller than the rest of the guys at the gym. Because of his size and weight, it's inevitable that he's going to end up in the corner or against the ropes.

I stopped short of mentioning the fatal blow, figuratively speaking of course. That's because no matter how deep into a corner Perry seems to find himself in, he's always managed to squeeze himself out of it. If he sustains his interest in boxing long enough, I foresee a rewarding coaching role for him. This is thanks to his capacity for solving problems at the drop of a coin. He always seems to be thinking one or two steps ahead of the next guy.

Indeed, Perry is one of the most composed guys I've ever seen walk into our gym. Before we wonder any further how he does it, let me reassure you that this chapter will show you how problems *can* be solved. And no further encouragement needs to be given to you to apply similar problem-solving techniques to your own life.

Composure's Role in Problem-Solving

In the meantime, you're probably still wondering: Why do we have so many problems in life? And why do they never seem to go away and leave us in peace? Come to think of it, problems do go away. Eventually. But usually through trial and error, and even a bit of luck. But no sooner has one problem left you when another has arrived to take its place.

Let me explain composure's role in *solving* problems, not wishing them away. Wishing that your problems go away will only lead to them either getting worse or coming back to bite you in the backside. It's another way of saying that unresolved problems remain if they're ignored. Whether as a team leader or a team player, a fully composed man doesn't take matters personally, not letting his emotions get in the way of his problem-solving capabilities.

The fully composed man is not afraid of walking into a challenge. He's not afraid of confrontation if it ever comes to that. Fearless he may be but I think his problem-solving abilities might have more to do with his ability to keep himself positive at all times, even when under pressure. The fully composed problem-solver is also a champion. That's because he's not going to utilize delaying tactics by acting decisively and making every moment count during his problem-solving opportunity. He will keep his shoulders back, and head held high, and hold himself accountable at every stage of the problem-solving exercise, even if the initial problem was not of his making or had nothing to do with him specifically.

It's too easy to cave into the temptation to just give up or walk away. But particularly if the problem is of your own making, where will that leave you? If you're not careful, you could find yourself out of a job. So, if you're going through a crisis right now, do your best to stay calm. Keep yourself together, and try to evaluate rationally what's really going on, and what's really gone wrong. It could turn out that the problem is a lot smaller than you make it out to be. By keeping yourself composed, you'll also be helping others to stay calm. You'll be helping to create a safe space in which no one needs to panic in the face of adversity.

But while you and your colleagues, friends, or family members seek to make improvements in your capacity to deal with and solve problems, the under-achiever, sore loser, and no-hoper will continue asking themselves: why? Why are we faced with so many problems? Why do we have to deal with them? Why can't others deal with them? Come to think of it, listening to these guys ask so many "why" questions reminds me so much of the "what-if" hole that those with a fixed mindset have chosen to dig themselves into.

The Underachiever

If he insisted on never listening to another line of good, growth-oriented advice, the fixed mindset underachiever would spend his entire life digging himself into what he likes to think is his safety zone. If he only does so much every day, there's less chance of him falling into a hole he won't be able to dig himself out of. Or so he likes to think. The underachiever is not prepared to set his sights higher than it needs to be. After all, if he aims any higher in life, he's bound to fall and fail hard. He doesn't want to set himself up for disappointment.

And so, life goes for the perennial underachiever, from one year into the next, never having to bother himself with other people's problems, to say nothing of his own. But if only he knew how much he was deluding himself, only to wake up one day to ask himself the one "what-if" question, alongside the "if only" questions that could turn out to be a significant turning point in his life. If only I had taken on more responsibilities in life? If only I had made an attempt to make something more of my life?

What if I wasn't so negative and so afraid of all life's challenges? Where would I be today?

Sadly, it's not hard to imagine why the so-called born loser is destined to fail in life if he chooses to never get out of bed in the morning and face his problems like any responsible man would. I think the term applied to such men is harsh and sometimes unfair. After all, there could be underlying influences that led to him being in such a state. As a child, he could have been treated rather badly by his parents. During his early teens or young adulthood years, there could have been a traumatic incident that caused him to want to keep a low profile, always hiding in the shadows of mainstream society.

Sadly, the shy guy fails to realize that just because he failed during one disastrous date, doesn't mean that he's going to fail again. He may have failed to realize at the time that that one single failure in his life, may not have been a reflection of who he was, and why he did what he did. Or what he didn't do. But even if he made mistakes that offended or hurt others, he must learn to accept the mistakes he made because if he can do that, he can only learn from them.

Sadly, the underachiever who isn't able to or prepared to make any progress in his life, often finds himself at the bottom of the food chain, just like the pushover I introduced to you in Chapter 5. It is at this point that I'd like to reprise what life is like when you're at the bottom of the food chain before moving on to great stories on how to deal with the problems we're all faced with in this world.

God help those who do find themselves at the bottom of the food chain, quite literally so, and through no fault of their own. But God help those who failed and allowed themselves to lapse to the bottom. We could help them but they can help themselves too. And of course, God helps those who help themselves. But by that, we don't mean those who help themselves to what others have achieved in life, usually through honest means.

One way or another, those that find themselves at the bottom of the food chain could very well find themselves with little food to eat. If they weren't able to manage their finances, they may have found themselves in a job that didn't pay them what they should have been worth. They were paid below the belt. They might not have been lazy or undeserving but perhaps did lack courage and never applied themselves enough to the "I" statement I demonstrated in Chapter 5. Unlike most men who seem to get away with murder—figurately speaking, of course—these poor men lacked the assertiveness required to get their way, whether fairly or not is beside the point.

The Solutionist

How many men, famous or known only to themselves, are good at solving problems? How many of these men do you know of who have the courage of their convictions and in all sincerity, will do their utmost best for someone else who's in a lot more trouble than he can help himself with? For that matter, how many women do you know of who can do similar great things? All things being equal in your life, how many solutionists do you know? Are you a solutionist?

And what is a solutionist in any case? A solutionist is a solver of problems, of that we can have little doubt. He is a problem-solver. He is also known as a fixer or issue resolver. He is someone who can act decisively in the middle of a conflict, deal with it, and resolve it. He is a guy who can make a plan. And she is someone who will go out of her way to help others out of their dilemmas. She is someone who is brave enough, and kind enough to help those less fortunate than herself.

Being a solutionist requires a positive state of mind. It is growth-oriented and is always able to look beyond the problems of the day. It has long-term objectives in mind which are usually designed around making life and all that it encompasses, better than it is in the present.

A Great Man Who Is Great at Solving Problems

A problem solver also has the ability to be inventive. Like the great Albert Einstein or even Leonardo da Vinci, he could apply a little science. But like the dramatists Oscar Wilde and William Shakespeare, and like the rock iconoclast, David Bowie, and even the war-time prime minister, writer, and painter Winston Churchill, he can apply a lot of art. Indeed, to be an effective problem-solver requires one to have an adaptive mind. But it does not require us to stay up until two, three, or even four in the morning, trying to solve the world's problems.

If your mind is as adaptive as the solutionist's is, you'll embrace challenges, and treat them as new learning opportunities for yourself, as well as others if you're a father, ice hockey captain, a four-star general or great leader of men. You'll welcome different perspectives to help reach amicable solutions to universal problems. You might obsess from time to time but will strive to be as pragmatic as possible, always willing to try out new angles in the event that previously proposed solutions have not yielded the desired outcomes.

In my mind, a true problem-solver is also a pragmatist. He also knows when it's time to take a step back and make full use of what is known as the three R's:

- Rest

- Recover

- Recharge

In the context of solving everyday problems, the pragmatist is a far cry from the under-achiever who chooses to duck under the radar and wish problems away or avoid them altogether. The pragmatist knows that he cannot solve everyone's problems every day, but he is exercising his emotional right to care about the problems others are going through and spare himself for another day to help work toward finding a solution to what they're experiencing. If not that, he's a remarkable leader who is going to teach them well on how to solve their own problems without stretching their hands out for hand-outs. The leader is going to give his followers a sense of what it feels like to be empowered.

An Opportunity for Growth

Where others see no hope, problem-solvers see growth. If not that, they see an opportunity for growth in almost every sphere of their lives. They've included others within this sphere too, of course. Even great men like Eisenhower and

Einstein will be the first to acknowledge that failures, along with successes, are not a zero-sum game but a realistic game of numerous trials, and numerous errors.

These are men who not only embraced opportunities to win battles and achieve breakthroughs but chose to do so with a great deal of responsibility, always sound in the knowledge that the decisions they made then, would have an impact on millions of lives in a different era. As the anointed leader of the Battle of Normandy, also known as Operation Overlord, Eisenhower had to be a master strategist to ensure that the united force of the Allies could defeat the might of fascism almost in one fell swoop. That mistakes were made and lives were lost is a matter of history but doesn't take away the fact that it could have turned out differently if the general didn't have his wits about him.

At almost every turn, Eisenhower knew he had to count on others for the success of the war. So too, the great Steve Jobs who knew that not only should opportunities for growth be grasped, but they should be created as well. Jobs was a masterful strategist too but significantly in his case, he couldn't get the original Apple Inc. board of directors to toe the line with him. As far as he was concerned, their mindsets were fixed, and he was having none of it. And the rest, as they say, is history, as far as one of the world's most valued brands goes.

Common Traits of the Masterful Strategist

As a keynote strategist in the business world, you'd have to be blind not to see the common traits of a masterful strategist. I train college-bound kids, and I write health, wellness, and mental health books, and I can even see some of the stand-out features of the corporate-minded, entrepreneurial, help-oriented thinking skills of a man who only wants to solve problems so that not only himself but others may benefit. Here's a list of great features that epitomize the masterful strategist:

- In spite of time being money, masterful strategists make time for thinking. No matter how busy the day is, they will guard whatever precious little time they've set aside for themselves to think.

- Masterful strategists are not only solitary thinkers. They'll make time to be in the company of others who, preferably, won't be thinking alike. Different levels of thinking are pooled together so that all can learn, grow, and develop.

239

- Masterful strategists keep themselves in the present but are thinking in the long-term. The decisions made, and the events of today that shape them, need to make a positive impact on the future, years from now.

- Different points of view are always welcomed. To make the cultivation thereof possible, masterful strategists will go out of their way to establish new relationships with others.

- Like Apple's Steve Jobs, masterful strategists are able to take a breather from their usual course of business and spot new trends always on the horizon. They also see what others are doing but want to make sure that whatever they're doing is working.

Life's Good

If nothing's working, then it's back to the drawing board, and the whole strategic process repeats itself, with a few strategic differences added in. The differences take note of what knowledge acquisition has brought to the table for the master strategist. In the meantime, life's pretty good for the composed strategist. Take the famous example of Jobs. Legend has it that he could lose his temper pretty easily when he lost his patience with engineers who, in his mind, weren't thinking out of the box. But I think it's safe to say that he made up for his intransigence by practicing Buddhist-inspired meditation.

The fact that he was one of the world's richest men back then didn't seem to bother him. And as far as we're concerned, money should not be regarded as a reward for solving the world's problems. Rather, we should be focusing on what we can gain from problem-solving intrinsic values, of which the following comes to mind:

- The problem-solver doesn't need to be told what to do when there's a crisis. He's already created an environment which allows him to address problems before they arrive. He doesn't have a crystal ball in front of him but does take an anticipatory approach to future events that might happen, and need to be fixed.

- While others are risk takers, the solutionist is also a risk solver. Having already anticipated future events, he has also developed cause-and effect relationships within the environment he's operating in. He has addressed probable causes, and while he's not a miracle worker, he can enable actions in the present to alter the likelihood of a future event occurring.

- The solutionist is always seeking to improve his performance capabilities, as well as that of others. He has helped to create an interdependent environment which enables others within his ambit to work together to solve more complex problems as and when they occur.

- A problem solved today is an opportunity created for the future. New measures are put in place to ensure that what happened previously doesn't need to reoccur in the future. But if it does, both he and his team will be better positioned to address the problem to hand.

Inherently, your ability to solve problems empowers you to identify and exploit opportunities within the environment you're working or living in. You have the ability to at least exert some control over your future, as well as that of others.

Cultivating Resilience in the Face of Adversity

The above environment would not have been possible if you, as a problem-solver, didn't have a belief that you could solve problems alone or with the help of others, if need be. You would not have been able to solve problems if you were lacking in composure. One important factor that allows you to keep your cool within an under-pressure environment is resilience. In this chapter, I've introduced you to great men from all walks of life who serve as role models for us to follow. These great men are not perfect, not by any means, and when they did make mistakes previously, they were able to learn from their mistakes and persevere with the objectives they set for themselves and others.

One of these great men was British Prime Minister Winston Churchill. Among the many great feats he became famous for, one seems to stand out. It was his gift of public speaking. He wasn't entirely spontaneous with his choice of words, and would literally spend hours rehearsing and practicing what he wanted to say to the public. At the height of arguably the greatest crisis to have occurred during the 20th century, Churchill said to those who would listen to him: Never, ever, ever give up.

It was as though he wasn't just speaking to the British people he represented as their prime minister. It was as though he was speaking to the entire world. Of course, he wasn't alone in his exhortations. Other great men played their part too, and if it wasn't for Franklin D. Roosevelt's efforts to get the American people behind him, who knows how history would have turned out?

Men like Churchill and Roosevelt, in spite of their personal challenges (Churchill suffered from depression, while Roosevelt was confined to a wheelchair), composed themselves well. Had they not done so, perhaps people wouldn't have been convinced to take the actions that were required to save the world from tyranny. And the resilience these men showed was surely a great example for all to follow.

How Composure Helps You to Overcome

At the height of adversity, composure helps you to overturn a bad situation. Composure allows you to instill a positive, can-do attitude. Everything that seemed impossible and hopeless to you before is now doable. Depending on how problematic your challenges have been, composure might not achieve a sought-after result but at least it would have brought you closer toward overcoming your challenges. Anxiety and worry don't disappear overnight because you must still work toward overcoming these mental challenges as well.

While learning how to overcome these mental challenges, composure teaches you to stay calm and focused, while at the same time keeping you productive. It makes no sense for you to drop everything you're supposed to be doing while under pressure to perform and produce. Doing nothing achieves nothing and the problems you're faced with only get worse.

Alongside resilience, you also need to exercise restraint. You cannot allow distressed emotions to get the better of you. You cannot allow impulsivity to lead you into a dark alley of bad habits from which it might become difficult to extract yourself from. Composure teaches you to replace negative thinking with rational, objective questions, such as: What must I really do to solve the problem that's before me? Being rational allows you to collect the information you need to help you make better decisions about what must be done, and what can be done.

Composure, influenced by rational thinking, allows you to say to yourself that all is well. If not that, you can realistically project that all will be well soon.

Resilience

If all is not yet well for you, there is always resilience, not resistance, always keeping in mind that challenges won't be overcome, and problems won't be solved if you insist on running away from them. Resilience will help you to persevere and not give up. In the previous chapter, I alluded to men like you and me being under pressure. This is something I could have told you at any time of the day, week, month, or year. Pressure is part of life but there is no reason why we need to go down under because of it.

Before I introduce you to the practice of resilience, I'd like you to take a moment to compose yourself. Don't allow yourself to feel overwhelmed by whatever it is that you are facing. You may think about past mistakes you may have made in the past. But think for a moment about this. Don't beat yourself about what you did or didn't do. Now is not the time to have regrets. Now is the time to learn from your mistakes. But while you do this, remind yourself once more that no matter how many improvements you've made in your life, mistakes will continue to be made.

It is part of being human. But what's even more remarkable about being human is that we all have the ability to bounce back and make things better than they were before.

That's also thanks to resilience, a characteristic streak we all have as human beings. For you it is now just a question of honing your ability to practice this must-have quality that you need to endure, overcome, and solve the problems you're faced with, whether they are of your own making or not.

What Is Resilience?

The American Psychological Association (APA) describes resilience as the process and outcome of successfully adapting your mind and body to challenging life experiences. It also provides you with the ability to be flexible in the way you behave, and adjusting to both external and internal demands. But where to begin? The APA also says that through the use of psychological research and qualified therapy practices, resources and skills associated with resilience can be cultivated and practiced. Elsewhere in this book, I mentioned that CBT or DBT could be introduced to help you cope.

Like DBT, CBT is a form of talk therapy that was primarily designed to treat a number of mental health conditions, including stress, anxiety, and depression. But there's no reason why it can't be used to help you deal with excessive drinking, eating irregularities (not eating enough or eating too much), marriage or family problems, or the pressures you face at work or school. CBT also introduces the patient to a number of strategies, of which the following appear to be the most common (APA):

- Learning to recognize negative thinking patterns that create problems.

- Gain a better understanding of behavioral patterns.

- Introduce problem-solving skills to help you cope with difficult situations.

- Face your fears instead of avoiding them.

- Use role-playing to better prepare you to deal with your problems, as well as your interactions with others.

- Learn to stay calm and relax both mind and body.

DBT, on the other hand, helps you to accept the reality of your circumstances. It also helps you to change the way you're thinking, and the way you approach your problems by chipping away at your bad habits and replacing them with healthier, proactive problem-solving habits. DBT was originally developed for people who are being treated for borderline personality disorders. As a form of talk therapy, it helps people who experience intense emotions.

How to Build Resilience and Use It

Both of the above therapy approaches can also be used to help build resilience and use it effectively. But whether you're working with a therapist or practicing a form of self-help therapy, building resilience requires time and patience. Lacking composure, this could have been a lonely and challenging time for you. Rest assured that the APA stresses the importance of building new connections during this challenging time of your life. It also requires you to prioritize relationships, in which case, you would want to rid yourself of toxic people and replace them with empathetic and understanding folks who can help you validate your feelings. The practical implications of building your resilience require you to observe the following four core components:

- Connection

- Health and wellness

- Healthy thinking

- Meaning

Along with setting aside negative thoughts, negative people, and negative or harmful areas or circumstances, building resilience encourages you to find a sense of purpose in your life. You can align this with your personal goals. At the same time, these goals need to be realistic. You will also be required to work toward them regularly and proactively. Being proactive in the way you approach everyday problems, to say nothing of those that could potentially make or break your life, requires you to acknowledge and accept your emotions during challenging times. Instead of wishing away a problem as you may have done previously, you're now taking the bull by the horns, and asking yourself what you can do to solve the problem you're faced with.

Perhaps the athlete training for the season-ending NCAA track and field championships or even the Olympic trials is one of the best examples that we can use to highlight the above explanation. After all, three or four months down the line, the athlete might injure himself, and have to start his training from scratch after making a full recovery. During this time, he cannot afford to lose his composure, and he certainly cannot rush his recovery. Doing so could have been counterproductive but on the chance that he's not able to make a full recovery, he simply has to accept his fate and start thinking about the future, preparing himself to grasp the next opportunity. Apart from accepting the changes that need to be made in your life, you also need to look for new opportunities of self-discovery. While discovering new things about yourself, you're also better positioned to learn from your past.

Learning From Your Mistakes

Learning from your past also allows you to learn from the mistakes you may have made in the past. Even so, no matter how well-composed you may become, you're still going to make mistakes, with or without pressure. There will always be moments of weakness that may cause you to take your eye off the ball. But such moments never need to be fatal. All it requires is a pragmatic, problem-solving approach laced with that can-do mentality I alluded to elsewhere in this book.

Begin by reassuring yourself that making a mistake is not the same as failing. Tell yourself that you are *not* a failure. Failure is the result of a wrong action while making a mistake *is* the wrong action. Making a mistake not only allows you to learn from it but fix it. Next, be a man and own up to the mistake that you've made, particularly if it has hurt or offended others.

Once you've done that, you're ready to reframe your mistake. You'll use this step as an opportunity to learn and develop. You'll also ditch any negativity you may have associated with the mistake you made and replace it with a pledge to become more knowledgeable and resilient.

Once you've acknowledged your mistake, you can start thinking about what you could do to prevent it from reoccurring. Review what went wrong. During this review process, you can analyze your mistake honestly and objectively by asking yourself the following questions:

- What was I trying to do?

- What went wrong?

- When did it go wrong?

- Why did it go wrong?

Finally, as you proceed toward your commitment to learn from your error, place no pressure on yourself. Remind yourself that should you ever repeat the mistake (chances should be good that this will become less probable over time), you are not a failure. Rather, review the progress you've made in maintaining your composure, and reward yourself for the effort you put into regaining your composure.

Strength in Adversity

What you choose to do in your free time is entirely up to you. One thing I wouldn't advocate is regular late nights out with the boys. Remember, you've still got work to do. There's another training day ahead or perhaps you need to keep your mind sharp for study time after dinner. Late-night drinking diminishes your ability to produce coherent thoughts. Even so, there's still strength in numbers. It's great to surround yourself with like-minded men who, apart from their interests, might be going through similar trials, whether it's a troublesome marriage or indeed, a drinking problem. The athlete I mentioned will be bearing this in mind. He disciplines himself to take good care of himself away from the track. At the same time, he knows that extracurricular activities will help take his mind off the pressure of training, and will still be able to make space for himself to enjoy himself, all within reason, of course.

When I talk to guys at the gym, I like to use the strength training metaphor when explaining how the "strength in adversity" philosophy works. Think about it this way. You're already under a lot of strain when you're lifting heavy weights. But from a motivational point of view, you're using your resilience as target practice. The target, of course, is to increase your strength. You reach your target under the weight of adversity. Use this opportunity to discover levels of resilience you never imagined you could achieve.

Keep in mind that adversity tests your resilience. But after each challenge has been surpassed, you become better equipped to handle the next one, which may even be bigger than the previous one. When you develop resilience, you're already cultivating a sense of inner strength and confidence that empowers you to deal with challenges with courage and determination.

Having strength in adversity forces you to confront your weaknesses. It also forces you to question your beliefs. On that point, I wouldn't like you to regard this as a negative in the sense that you're now going to subject yourself to doubt. Rather, I'd use this questioning phase as an opportunity to reassess your priorities in life. If this requires you to step out of your comfort zone, then so be it.

How to Build and Maintain a Growth Mindset

The discovery of our inner strength is reminiscent of a growth mindset. The growth mindset encourages us to face our fears and take on the challenges we face head-on like young David with nothing more than a slingshot and a few pebbles to take on the giant warrior, Goliath. Of course, reading the story of David vs. Goliath, we appreciate that David's got a lot more on his side that Goliath hasn't seen. The young shepherd and future king had faith. He also believed solidly that he would slay the giant with one single shot to the forehead. At the same time, he allowed adversity to push him beyond perceived limits.

Let me close this significant chapter by introducing you to nine steps that can take you to the top of your growth trajectory. Begin by recognizing the fixed mindset traps you may be faced with against the tide of adversity. Recognize and acknowledge that these are ingrained beliefs that tell you that your abilities are limited and cannot be changed.

Secondly, embrace the challenges you're faced with. Never, ever run away from them but by all means, ask for help to deal with the challenges you're faced with. Asking for help forms part of the seventh and eighth steps that form part of your mindset growth. In the meantime, treat each challenge that you're faced with as a puzzle to be solved. Treat each challenge as a game that you can and must win. To help you get this far on this trajectory, don't fear failure.

Remember, you're not a failure, nor will you ever be. You merely make mistakes, just like everyone else. But you learn from them. Remember to treat failure as a learning experience. It is just another stepping stone toward your goals in life, in spite of the challenges you're faced with. The learning curve forms part of the fifth step toward growing a positive mindset. In the meantime, exercise patience, endurance, and yes, resilience too, by valuing the effort you're putting into the work required of you.

You can grow to love learning, just like I do. The positive learning experience requires just three things: to be curious, always seeking new knowledge, and resiliently steadying yourself to improve. This trajectory is also characteristic of the sixth step in the growth mindset trajectory. It is here that you're also cultivating persistence. Simply put, you never, ever, ever give up, no matter how hard the challenges are for you.

Sometimes, you can also give yourself a break. In the context of this exercise, take up the opportunity to seek constructive feedback. No doubt you'll be expecting positive feedback. After all, isn't this what is required of the growth mindset: to be positive? Don't worry if you've been criticized because if you've surrounded yourself with growth-oriented men, the criticism you receive is likely to be constructive. It is information you can use to positively develop yourself further.

On that note, value the experience of surrounding yourself with like-minded men (and women too) who are available to provide you with support, words of advice, and even stronger words of encouragement for you to succeed and overcome. And when you do achieve small, incremental milestones, don't forget to include them in your victory celebrations. All within reason, of course.

The harsh reality is as clear as daylight. No one likes a loser. While I disapprove of this weakness, I accept it as a fallible feature of human nature. I've also come to value and appreciate why women prefer being embraced by successful men rather than so-called crybabies. In this sense, the "cowboys don't cry" motif holds water. Because it's in their nature, women need to be reassured that they're safe. It's not as though they're lacking composure themselves, women or even young children for that matter, need constant reassurance that they're doing the right thing.

Workplace employees certainly have that going for them when they look up to their supervisor for the go-ahead to down tools to protest a raft of unfair decisions taken by top management. They can do that because not for nothing is their supervisor but their team leader as well. Leading a team is something the great Wayne Gretzky knows well. This is an aspect of composure we'll be talking about in the next chapter.

8. Leadership

Bert the Boss fired Jack. Owing to Jack's lack of performance, absence from work that went well beyond the time allowed, poor attitude, and bad rapport with the department's staff members, Bert felt justified in firing Jack. Personally, he had had enough of Jack's antics, and it took an untold toll on his personal life as well. He had long prided himself on being able to work the nine-to-five beat, with no need for overtime. But ever since Jack arrived, Bert had to spend more and more time at his desk after five, picking up the pieces and correcting Jack's mistakes.

And those were the good days when Jack actually decided to turn up. What happened on all those days when Jack wasn't at his desk? Bert had no alternative but to delegate the remainder of Jack's tasks to other staff members. Initially, they accepted this with grace. They were, after all, part of a team, and when one team member fell down, it was incumbent on the rest of the team to help pick up the pieces. But it went on for months. They had had enough.

They lodged one complaint after the next, but all Bert did was brush them aside and reassure them that all would be well soon. Soon, it was the next year. By that time, staff members weren't showing the enthusiasm for work that they did when they first filed into Bert's office, one by one. Salary increases were promised but never delivered. If there were any increases at all, they were minuscule compared to what the rest of the company was being given. The last straw appeared to be when management notified Bert that both he and his staff would not be receiving end-of-year bonuses.

Simply put, the numbers were unsatisfactory. Bert was given grace. He was given the next financial year to correct these numbers. But if he didn't deliver—as he promised he would—he would have to be shown the door as well. No doubt, Bert was under a lot of pressure. But whose fault was that?

Both you and I surely know the answer to that question.

The Weak Leader

Undoubtedly, Bert was to blame for his department's poor performance. He was, after all, the department's supervisor. In other companies, the title given to a man in his position is that of a team leader. But given what we have learned so far about Bert's performance, it doesn't look like he had the credentials of a leader. If we have to acknowledge that he was indeed a leader of men and women, we can say, without any doubt, that he was a *bad leader*, never mind a weak leader.

While he never attempted to "cook the books," the thought did cross his mind. Numerous times. What he could do with the extra cash, he had to wonder. But it wasn't as though he wasn't earning a decent salary. He was given similar packages to the company's other supervisors. What he did with the money he earned is nobody's business. He was in debt, no doubt about that. He was in debt to the staff members who made many sacrifices to cover his back.

Questions had to be asked. Questions were asked. Staff members counted on him for advice to help them out of difficult situations. Questions were asked about what needed to be done. How can I canvass my client for more business, even though I haven't delivered a satisfactory performance?

How can I justify price increases, even though the service delivery was less than satisfactory? How can we improve on last year's performance and beat the department next door?

Bert had no answers to these, and numerous other questions. Only excuses. He was weak and indecisive. He was never clear-headed, and simply followed orders from upstairs and delivered orders across the floor. Sometimes, out of sheer desperation, he would even make threats. Needless to say, this had a detrimental impact on staff morale, and after Jack was fired, some of them had to wonder: Will I be next?

For the best part of the work day, if it could be called that, Bert would shut his office door and draw the blinds. Nobody knew what he was doing behind closed doors.

What Happens to Weak Leaders?

It doesn't matter whether you're a dishonest or decent man, if you're a weak leader, you could be fired. If not, you could find yourself fortunate to be demoted. It is, after all, a chance for you to start again. I believe that everyone deserves second chances, even a third chance if it comes to that. But in the context of this section, there is a conundrum facing the demoted weak leader. Unable to compose himself, and apply his mind to his new position, doing tasks that he should have mastered by now, he now has to face the humiliation of being demoted.

His reputation is in tatters, and not able to concentrate on the job in front of him, he continues to wonder what others are saying behind his back. Quite frankly, I don't think he likes his job, and for that matter, he more than likely didn't like his leadership position. It's not because of a lack of interest in the work he was doing, it's just that he couldn't handle the pressure he was faced with. You could also acknowledge that even if you're a tough-minded, thick-skinned individual, you don't enjoy pressure either.

But pressure is a fact of life that we're all learning to come to terms with. Sadly, for the weak leader, he doesn't appear to have grasped the consequences of his insecurity and indecisiveness, to say nothing about his poor example. If he's still holding a leadership position, staff morale has, more than likely, sunk to an all-time low. Productivity levels drop as well, and out the window goes the chances of the company he represents making a profit that measures up to growth for the company.

If expectations are set at all, they are unclearly projected by the weak leader. Staff may scratch their heads wondering what it is he expects from them. Staff members may well be hardworking men and women but if they're unclear about their roles and targets, productivity levels may well continue to falter. For staff members who cherish the time spent with their families, particularly when the pressure starts to mount at work, the temptation is always there to be absent from work. A weak leader lacks the firmness to combat this form of ill-discipline.

The Problems Weak Leaders Must Face

It gets worse for the weak leader and his staff. Their customers have started to notice. The quality of the products or services expected by them drops to the point that they have no choice but to explore alternatives. It doesn't matter how long the customers have been on the company's books, loyalty counts for very little these days.

In the line of fire, insecure and indecisive weak leaders, particularly those that are thin-skinned, may feel as though they are all alone in the world. Everyone is out to get them. In their line of work, there are no friends, only enemies. Lacking political tact or ingenuity, such leaders may not even be familiar with the well-known term "frenemies." It is not so much a case of keeping your enemies close to you so that you can be aware of their every move, it's more a case of being able to co-operate with your rivals. Trade-offs, and the proverbial scratching of backs, are irksome to weak leaders.

Come to think of it, weak leaders *do* make promises they cannot keep or have no intention of keeping. Weak leaders don't appear to appreciate that the problems they're faced with every day are also universal. Indeed, competent, effective leaders face them as well. But as true leaders in every sense of the word, they don't see problems in front of them, "only" challenges. You might be familiar with this form of business-speak. It attempts to reassure followers that problems are never as bad as they may seem, and can be, and will be, resolved forthwith.

No doubt about it, weak leaders may have gone to business school, and like Charles, finished with flying colors. They could turn on the charm for just a short while in order to ace their interviews and secure their respective positions. But after just a few months in their positions, they begin to show their true colors. They may well be managers of men and women. But they are not leaders.

But if we insist on calling them weak leaders, we can at least agree that they usually lack vision, and are never a source of inspiration to others.

Leadership Is Not for the Faint-Hearted

Leadership is damn hard work. It's definitely not for the faint-hearted. So, if you have any aspirations in this direction, you had better brace yourself. Even with your best preparations in hand, it could be a bumpy ride ahead for you. Even if you're starting up a small business—a small online publishing company or a downtown coffee shop—you still need to brush up on your leadership skills.

The harsh reality, if it can be called that, of running a small service-oriented business where all you want to do is please your customers and earn a modest to decent income from doing so, is that you're still going to have to deal with employees who, working on a minimum wage might not be as motivated as you.

Operating within the confines of labor law, you hire, and you fire. Hiring staff is hard enough, having to sift through your best possible candidates. But firing staff members, even if your actions are justified and necessary, can be heart-breaking if you're a faint-hearted artist who never experienced the intricacies of entrepreneurship before. You might be able to inspire yourself to create something that your customers will love, but inspiring your staff members is quite a different story altogether.

To inspire them, you need to put all your energy and enthusiasm into the effort. You already appreciate the value you've created, but getting new staff members to believe in your plans for the small business is never easy. After all, you don't necessarily have what is known as the gift of the gab, not used to speaking with confidence to strangers perhaps. But you're a sincere, hardworking individual. What's not there to like? The harsh reality of being a strong leader is that sometimes, you have to give your personality a complete overhaul, metamorphosing from Mr. Nice Guy to Mr. Tough Guy. In leadership, you have to be tough, even when it hurts.

Indeed, while I hate rejection, I also know what it feels like to say no.

The Top Dog

The top dog is at the top of the food chain. He eats as and when he pleases. He has an intimidating bark but boy, can he bite too! If it's necessary, he can instill fear in others. Since the prehistoric era, there has always been a top dog, otherwise known as the alpha male. But thankfully, things have changed. Good, strong, effective leadership also requires honesty and integrity.

Unexpectedly forced into one of the most demanding but responsible jobs in the world after his long-term predecessor died, Harry S. Truman famously remarked that "the buck stops here." What he was essentially saying is that as Commander in Chief, while doing everything within his powers to serve and protect the people he represents, he will take full responsibility for any mistakes made. It's such a shame that so many of today's leaders-corrupt businessmen and morally corrupt politicians alike-have misinterpreted Truman's motto.

They take what is not theirs. They take the credit for what others have achieved. They speak ill of others.

But no, our top dog is having none of it. If there are any such leaders on his team, he'll most definitely fire them. Then again, if it was up to him, he would never have hired them in the first place. To get where he is in life, he has taken the time and effort to get to know people, how their minds work, and what they're capable of. That said, he can give the order and it will be done as demanded. But his followers deliver willingly. They're happy to do as he says because he's treated them well and led by example.

He might be an empath. But being so does not make him a "softy." Even so, he's still brave and courageous enough to fight the good fight on behalf of the team. Finally, the top dog is fully aware of the importance of developing his team. Even assuming that he was only thinking of himself, he knows full well that he wouldn't be successful if it wasn't for those who follow him. And they know that his success could be their success too.

Leadership Vulnerability

Leadership vulnerability is not the same as leadership weakness. Let me explain. In my long experience of being a leader in one capacity or another, usually down at the gym where I still give a lot of my time, vulnerability in a leader is appreciated a lot more among his followers than the traditionally assertive nature of the traditional boss who spends most of his time delegating tasks.

Vulnerability in a leader is expressive in the sense that you're leaving yourself wide open, willing to show and express emotion if you feel that it is warranted. I've found that it's a great way to build trust among members of my team. Leadership vulnerability also paves the way toward building stronger relationships with each member of the team.

But when you express yourself emotionally, you're not prone to angry outbursts when things aren't going your way. Rather, your vulnerability allows you to draw yourself closer to each team member, placing yourself in a good position to assign tasks to those who show that they're ready to take on more responsibilities. Vulnerability allows you to connect more effectively with your team, showing compassion, and even expressing joy when the team or a member of the team has won a small victory. Finally, the following features highlight the power of vulnerability as a leader:

- Trust is increased. Also, trustworthiness allows everyone to show their authentic side.

- There's better employee engagement. Thanks to the trust you've built as a vulnerable leader, employees are willing to show up on time and be relied upon.

- The vulnerable leader's qualities allow him to build more productive teams. Because of the open work environment, conflicts, and problems, whenever they arise, are solved more quickly.

- Employees or team members feel that they're in a safe emotional space.

- The vulnerable leader's courage extends to the team. Following his example, they become more courageous too. Through increased emotional intelligence and creativity, there's also a willingness to take risks.

When you become more vulnerable as a leader, you're able to show more empathy and compassion. A strong leader lets his followers know in no uncertain terms that they are cared for and can come to him for help. Strong, vulnerable leadership encourages an open-door policy, all within reason, of course.

Leadership Strength

Strong leaders need to show discipline. Discussing problems or what you did over the weekend (always good for building morale) has its time and place in the work environment. But without the need to boss people around, the strong leader reminds his team that there's still work to be done. While vulnerability remains an unknown quality to most managers and their employees, strong leadership should be valued and respected, rather than feared.

Strong but vulnerable leaders in all walks of life have the capacity to become great leaders. Also, being vulnerable doesn't mean that you're lacking composure. On the contrary, an honest leader is not afraid to show a side of himself that could be perceived as a weakness. In the meantime, take to heart the following qualities that contribute toward the making of a great leader:

- **Authenticity**: Showing your followers that there's a genuine side to you reassures them that you won't keep anything from them. Being honest and open toward

272

others shows them that you can relate to similar struggles that they might be going through, and go one step further toward helping them to help themselves.

- **Compassion**: Compassion allows you to not only understand others but to appreciate them as well. As a great leader, you will show your appreciation to others for the work they've done for the team. Compassion allows you to be at the coalface with your team, rather than isolating yourself within the four walls of your office.

- **Curiosity**: Your curiosity allows both you and the team to learn and grow. Your leadership vulnerability also allows you to build stronger cultures. There is respect and understanding for each member of the team, no matter what differences there are. You use your curiosity to promote creative thinking on how to leverage resources in new, original ways.

- **Grace**: Kindness and goodwill need to be shared with each member of the team to help them cope in a high pressure environment. Instead of hiding away in fear, they're allowed to grow. Everyone knows that mistakes could be made but there is nothing to fear from them, particularly since they can all learn from them, just as you have.

The Power of Community

All of the above qualities of an engaged, composed leader should have already provided you with an awareness that nothing of value can be achieved without the help of others. This doesn't mean that you're in a helpless position and completely dependent on others. As a leader or a work-from-home entrepreneur (with you as the sole employee), you don't need to be at the mercy of others either. But in an ideal environment, there can be nothing more valuable than the power of the community.

It is an ideal worth striving for. I believe that the power of the community is potentially so strong within us that it even allows us to work with our rivals. But if you've made enemies during your journey, there's no reason why you cannot break bread with them as well. Making the first offer of a handshake as a peace offering and proposal to open a dialogue is one of the finest qualities of a leader I've witnessed to date.

A good, experienced leader may have grown with wisdom. But in my personal experience, collective or shared wisdom could open more doors for you. Even if you were in no position to surround yourself with others, as happened during a critical stage of my life, there are always books. There is the social media environment as well. You can enrich yourself through others. And as a leader, you can motivate others as well.

When you're working under pressure or pushing yourself too hard, burnout could be inevitable. It becomes tempting to give up on what you're doing but if you have surrounded yourself with others who are there to motivate and support you, you don't want to appear weak to them, and will subconsciously make yourself accountable to them, always keeping them up to date on the progress you're making. Such is the power of the community. There is also the power of composure, which is particularly important for an aspirant leader like yourself.

Displaying Composure as a Leader

Whether working as a by-the-book manager or supervisor, or as a model leader, you're accountable to others, whether you like it or not. Whether from your employees or fellow team members, or boardroom management, expectations are always high for you to deliver sought-after results on time. People are expecting you to be a beacon of strength and resilience for them. While you allow yourself to be vulnerable, you still need to keep yourself calm and composed. You need to show others that you have the inner strength to deal with the challenges you're faced with, with confidence.

In leadership, composure requires you to display a sense of calm, control, and equilibrium toward others. You are expected to keep yourself steady under pressure and make rational, sometimes even thought-provoking decisions for the benefit of others. With such high expectations riding on your shoulders, there is still no reason why you need to buckle under pressure. You and your team can still go places. You can still inspire confidence in others.

But as an aspirant leader, there is still work to be done. Indeed, the true leader also knows that he has to continue working to maintain his composure as well. After all, he's still vulnerable, and he's still human. As I've mentioned elsewhere in this book, mindfulness and self-awareness practices are cornerstones of keeping your composure. But so too, the keeping of healthy habits. This is something we'll be discussing in the final chapter. In the meantime, don't let setbacks rule your life. And remember always to ask for help, guidance, and advice whenever you feel as though you need it.

I know asking for help can be difficult sometimes when the setbacks of life have dealt your self-esteem a blow. But remember that there's no shame in asking. People won't think any differently of you if you do. And the more you persevere, the closer you'll come to seeking the definitive answers you're looking for. I also believe that people will be more amenable to you if you're someone who leads or lives by example. Indeed, they may well aspire to inherit some of your best qualities which you've yet to notice. I have said this before, while you reflect on your weaknesses, you need to think seriously about your strengths and dig a little deeper to see how you could exploit them.

Importance of Composure for Leaders

In order to stress the importance of composure for leaders, we need to cover the ground we've covered previously. This is not repeat work or a form of learning by rote. In fact, make use of your journaling time to reflect on the following fine qualities of a composed leader:

- As a composed leader, you are calm and poised. You are not intimidated by external pressures. Your level-headed approach to the pressure-cooker environment helps to create an atmosphere of stability for the rest of the team.

- Emotionally and physically, you are in control. You have come to understand your workplace reactions and can adjust them as and when needed, setting an example for the rest of the team to emulate.

- Your ability to compose yourself well under pressure helps you to produce cognitive excellence. In other words, you think clearly, make good decisions, and can solve problems efficiently.

- As a competent, confident, and composed leader, you've earned the trust of those who follow you. And while they continue to look to you for guidance and advice, you feel no pressure and embrace the dependence.

Leading by Example

As a sports team leader, entrepreneur, business leader, or even a clergyman or politician, what does it take to be an effective leader? What does it take to lead by example? To begin: instead of ordering someone to do something, propose to him that you can help him complete the task as a fellow team member. You can be the shot-stopper, freeing your teammate with more room to maneuver on the wings before passing to the forward for him to strike.

If not, you can certainly guide your team from the sidelines. They follow your lead, not because you demand them to deliver excellence but because you're an embodiment of that excellence. Leading by example, you value the contributions being made by your fellow team members. You don't keep this to yourself; you share it with the team. Because they're working hard on your behalf, you pitch in to help them as well. As unusual as this scenario may look to you at this point in time, it is how you express value for the work being done.

Leading by example, you get involved, and you even put others before you. No, it's not the same as Napoleon sending hundreds of working-class men to their deaths while he reviews events from the back of the battlefield. It's more like Alexander the Great leading the charge from the front. Even so, both men had the gift of being able to motivate and inspire. So too Churchill, as you'll recall from this and previous chapters.

Perhaps that's also the difference between great leaders and weak leaders: great leaders don't need to micromanage. Great leaders allow their followers to complete their tasks in ways that fit their abilities, and in ways that they're comfortable with, just as long as the rules of the game are being followed. This ability to restrain himself from interfering with the work his followers are attempting to complete also shows that he is flexible.

But every once in a while, he will chip in and reorder the workshop. As far as he is concerned, tasks need to be shared equitably, and commensurate with abilities. He knows this is necessary because he'd like to avoid one or more workers succumbing to burnout. Even so, every worker knows what's expected of them. After all, their supervisor has been able to effectively communicate this to them. At the same time, he has listened to them, not only for meaning but for understanding as well.

Keep Your Cards Close to Your Chest and Stay Calm Under Pressure

Here's another set of reminders you need to work through if you'd like to do well as a leader someday. This takes into account that in life, pressure is inevitable. However, because the responsibilities given to leaders are greater for them than for others who choose to follow, the pressure may be greater. That being said, the journal exercise, as one of your regular self-care tools, becomes effective. You can use your journaling time to self-reflect. In the context of simulating a leadership position, you'll need to regularly assess your ability to compose yourself in different situations. It is during this reflection time that you'll need to think about the triggers that cause you to remain stressed or anxious, and devise strategies to address these stress-inducing situations.

Over time, you'll learn how to adapt and evolve through the experiences you've had. If you've been faced with a stressful situation, you'll embrace it as an opportunity to strengthen your composure. All setbacks endured are learning experiences, and the lessons you've learned from them will stand you in good stead for a leadership position in the future. I do, however, believe that the work/life experience can be enhanced further through others. No, they won't necessarily be telling you what to do. As a potential leader, you need to learn how to make your own decisions. However, the decisions you make can be influenced by the support and constructive feedback you've received from your peers and/or mentors.

There is, of course, only so much your mentors can do for you. The rest is still up to you, and again, can include home-based self-help practices such as mindful meditation or walking exercises. Teach yourself the art of proper time management as well. The ability to practice good time management will help reduce the pressure of demanding deadlines. It will also strengthen your ability to manage tasks with composure, just as long as you continue to prioritize, set realistic goals, and delegate tasks whenever necessary. All good and well that you believe in leading by example, just like I do, but the harsh reality remains: You cannot do everything yourself.

That said, you need to consider the benefits that outsourcing could bring to your future business. In the meantime, keep your cards close to your chest. What do we mean by this expression? Undoubtedly, through *The Art of Composure*, as well as other resources, you'll be making steady progress in the direction you want to go. With more composure, you'll have a better focus on what you want to achieve. Your plans are made, and they're bold. But they're also on hold until such time you've met up with the right collaborators. They could be your future business partners. Your rivals, on the other hand, known and unknown to you, will be none the wiser. Why? Because you've kept your cards close to your chest.

The Importance of Outsourcing

If you started your own small business, would it help if you outsourced some of your service offerings? Would it help your work-from-home business if you got someone online to provide you with, and help manage a user-friendly bookkeeping service? Would it help if you could utilize the services of a smart-and-savvy but experienced sales rep to canvas for new business while you get on with your business of preparing scrumptious meals or building bespoke dining room tables and chairs? Of course it would. After all, you cannot do everything yourself. Also, the few employees you need to utilize for the day-to-day running of the business, may not have the skills required, to say nothing of the time that may be taken away from their usual tasks, to carry out the new tasks you'd like to implement to make your business more viable and competitive.

Outsourcing is not a reflection of weakness, nor does it suggest that you're incapable of managing your business. Rather, it shows that you're also realistic enough to take pragmatic measures to save time and money. After all, time *is* money.

Outsourcing was first recognized as a formal business strategy in 1989. From a business point of view, outsourcing is a process of hiring third parties to conduct services that may already have been carried out by the company. The company's primary motivations for utilizing this type of service were to cut labor costs and focus on the core operations of the business.

Work could be completed by another person, allowing the business owner to focus on more important tasks. My concern remains this: will the outsourced work be as good as my own? Will we be able to communicate effectively with our new service providers? Do we need to be concerned about security threats in an environment where multiple parties could have access to our sensitive information?

Setting aside such concerns for now, let's close this section with the positives. Outsourcing may allow us to become more flexible and efficient in the way we conduct our business affairs. And within the company, there may be new opportunities to only utilize the best available talent.

Setbacks Should Never Let You Down

If you've been a business owner for a while, don't treat the inevitability of outsourcing, and the initial costs associated with the service, as a setback. Treat this event as an opportunity to grow your company even further. When changes need to be made to the way we earn our keep, we could expect salary adjustments. When changes need to be made to our personal lives, we should expect some discomfort. But if your attitude is positive, you should be able to take new birth pains in your stride.

You are on a new growth trajectory. It is also an opportunity for you to learn new things about yourself. You can also take advantage of learning from others. During this time, you should feel free to ask as many questions as you wish about what you're going through. After all, you may never know what to do next if you don't ask. Setbacks, and the changes they may require, should be seen as a new opportunity to connect with new people. New faces should project positivity. You should be able to take comfort in their example, and as you get to know them, trust them a little more than you would have trusted people in the past.

Trust also allows you to open up to others. You can make yourself accountable to them. Ask them for advice. Ask them for feedback. But don't take it personally when criticism is given. If you've surrounded yourself with good people, the criticism you receive should be constructive. Most importantly, you need to remind yourself to be responsible and take good care of yourself. If you come from a background of low self-esteem, always lacking confidence in your abilities as a man, you need to be at your best to manage the new changes in your life, whether great or small. Let's close this section with a few highlights of how a composed leader is able to conduct himself under high-pressure circumstances:

- A composed leader acts decisively.

- He always projects a positive attitude toward others.

- His followers can see that he's focused and goal-oriented.

- They know that their leader can be trusted.

- A composed leader is able to produce better results, particularly during conflict situations.

- He preserves his integrity, maintains his self-control, and is able to build confidence in others.

You Are as Strong as Your Weakest Member

I like to use fitness training as a metaphor for helping us to root out the weeds in our garden of growth. They are an impediment to the beauty we'd like to project. If they're not rooted out, they can invade the space of the good plants, causing them to wither. A good-looking pair of biceps is all good and well. It will certainly attract the notice of the opposite sex. But big, bulging muscles are hardly useful if they don't have the strength to match it. You won't be in a good place to act as a knight in shining armor to assist your damsel in distress in times of danger.

You also need strong support when you're expected to lift heavy weights in the construction yard. So, back at the gym, you'll want to focus on developing your thighs and calf muscles, as well as other areas of your body. What you're seeking to achieve is all-round cardiovascular fitness. In order to achieve that, mental strength and fitness is required as well. Back in the construction yard, acting as a supervisor on your shift, it goes without saying that you need to surround yourself with a strong team of men, all of whom should be capable of carrying out the tasks delegated to them.

As a decent man, you'll want to give every lad who approaches you for a job to help put food on the table, a fair opportunity. While your mind remains focused on assembling the best possible team, there is surely a place for one or two new arrivals who've never had experience in the construction business. As decent, well-groomed, and composed men themselves, they surely deserve an opportunity. But in order to make sure that they become useful members of the team, you'd have to make sure that they are adequately trained.

The Importance of Having a Strong Team Onboard

Having a strong team on board the ship will ensure that as many lives as possible will be saved in the event that the ship enters unchartered waters, and is sinking. The captain, as leader of the crew, will make sure that this happens after employing every rule of effective crisis management. And by the time the last man, woman, or child is safely overboard, the captain will proceed to rescue himself. As onerous as this tale may seem, I always find it inspirational. It is the epitome of strong leadership. But it might not have been possible if it weren't for his strong team.

Each team member brings on board his own set of skills and strengths. Every man has his place but when everyone works together as a team, everyone has an opportunity to learn from each other. In times of crisis, team members can rely on each other for support if their leader has his hands full of unique responsibilities which only he can carry out. New challenges will emerge but after each previous crisis has been resolved, the team will be better equipped to deal with these challenges. They will continue to improve their efficiency and will continue to be as productive as possible.

When a strong team works together, their responses to instructions will be clearer and on-point. Their willingness to collaborate well together, ensures that their better-understood goals are achieved successfully. Problems are always solved on time. Everyone on the team is motivated. Along with the diverse skills and strengths, it also helps to have a field of interests and backgrounds that are as diverse as the skills and strengths as well.

Several benefits accrue to the leader who has the acumen to assemble an exemplary team, namely better communication amongst team members, better efficiency, emotional support, and even healthy competition. The healthy competition is not designed to allow individuals to outmaneuver each other. Rather, it's a useful motivational tool that encourages each member of the team to achieve his best. At the end of the day, it is the team that benefits. Individual members of the team are reminded of their unique place in the team when everyone clubs together to celebrate each other's successes.

How to Strengthen Your Team

As a leader, the onus is on you to ensure that everyone communicates well together. During crises, make sure that you and your team focus on the problem, not on the person who may have caused the problem. If you feel obligated to communicate on a one-on-one basis, make sure that the message you're delivering carries equal weight to each member of the team. But in good times, validate each other's contributions, and always remember to complement good ideas or suggestions.

If there is enough room for competition amongst the team, make sure that you've provided incentives to motivate the competitive streak. But center these incentives on shared objectives. Set clear objectives to ensure that each team member knows what's expected of him. But as clear as these objectives are, make sure that the goals you're targeting are realistic and achievable. As has been the case for you throughout this book, the point is to motivate your team, not overwhelm them.

For new team members, make sure that you've given them enough time to acclimate to your progressive work environment by setting them straightforward objectives that are never onerous. You don't want to lose these promising young players by allowing them to doubt themselves and question their abilities so early in the game.

At the same time, you don't want the bar to be set too low. Tasks easily completed, and early knock-off times (as a reward for finishing work early), don't inspire workers to improve their performance rates, going forward.

Continue raising the momentum for your established players, empowering them to make important decisions. Trusting them to do this, could also relieve you of a few decision-making responsibilities. Remember, you are all adults in the room, and there's no room for babysitting. Those who aren't entrusted with decision-making responsibilities should always be free to share new ideas. It helps to make everyone feel invested and a permanent but important part of a strong team.

At this stage, while you're still working toward elevating your composure to allow you to stay strong in tight situations, I see no reason why I can't motivate you to continue aiming high, no matter what your hopes, dreams, and goals in life are. This will be a subject we'll talk about in the final chapter. Essentially, it's about improving your ability to master the art of composure.

9. Mastering the Art of Composure

Throughout this book, you have been given suggestions on how to regain your composure in all areas of your life. I have provided you with different scenarios, from the school playground to the workplace. You have been provided with suggestions on how to maintain your composure throughout, in both good and bad times. But in this final chapter, I'd like you to start thinking about going even further.

Remember what was said about the fixed mindset? It goes no further than it needs to. Or so it thinks. Life goes by for the man with a fixed mindset. He goes nowhere in life. He achieves nothing, is never promoted, and of course, is never adequately remunerated. He lacks the courage to speak up for himself. He is too scared to make justifiable demands. He can't stand up for others, let alone for himself.

At the bottom of the food chain, he could end up as a basket case, if he's not careful. I don't know about you but this is not the way I would like to live. Rather, I'd like to keep on developing my growth mindset so that I can achieve my goals without fear of failure. I'd like you to do the same too.

Aim High

I have noticed in my not-too-distant past that my personal ambition had gotten in the way of others in the sense that it made them feel uncomfortable. They are not my rivals, competitors, or enemies. They are family members and close associates who would hate to see me fail. Yes, I admit, I failed myself—and others—in the past. Then again, I do recall my wise dad reminding me that I didn't let others down, only myself. He also reassured me that there was no shame in failing, particularly if I had given my ambitions, however misguided they may have been in the past, my best shot like a cool Larry Bird toss at a 6a.m. training session.

I am not a basket case, and neither are you. And come hell or high water, we are going to succeed in life. Take yourself where you've never been before. If you never try, you'll never know what it feels like to be closer to the top of the food chain.

Aiming high does, however, require some introspection. Rationality tells us that if we start small, we're not necessarily lacking ambition, we're being cautious. We are setting small, realistic goals that we know or believe we can achieve.

Forget Goals, Focus on Systems

Another reason why NHL legend—Wayne Gretzky—could score more wins than losses was because he always had a system in place. Focusing on that, he could also orient his team to follow the system. The system requires patience because goals may not be scored in the first quarter. Goals may not be scored in the second quarter either. If necessary, it may only be scored at the death.

One of the greatest football coaches of all time certainly had a system in place. How else could Sir Alex Ferguson win 13 Premier League titles, 5 FA Cups, and 2 European Champions League titles? One of the trademark feats of his Man Utd squads was that they were always able to come from behind and snatch victory at the death. Indeed, arguably the most famous victory must surely have been the 1999 Champions League final against Germany's Bayern Munich.

They scored early and led for most of the match. But two minutes from time, Man Utd delivered the killer blows. Ferguson and his lads aimed high. Winning the European Cup was their holy grail. They achieved it. But to do so, even under dramatic circumstances, they had to have a system in place.

Don't Overwhelm Yourself with Too Many Goals

So that you don't muddle yourself during your planning and preparation phase, first write down all the goals you currently have in mind. So that you don't set yourself up for disappointment later on, don't set goals that, realistically, you might not be able to achieve. If you have goals in mind, you also need to set realistic timeframes. So that you're not distracted from your journey, have the courage to say no to those who may wish to place unreasonable demands on your shoulders.

The tasks you've set for yourself in writing can be prioritized. While you distance yourself from those that cannot be completed in the short-term, you can create more space to complete those that need to be completed in the current month of business. Break down these tasks into smaller increments. This allows you to become better organized. You can plan your tasks more effectively, and if time is of the essence, you can schedule yourself for quicker turnaround times.

But do not let speed diminish the quality of your work. Always pace yourself well, and discipline yourself to take regular breaks from your desk or workshop table. Think of it this way: The marathoner who breaks away from the leading pack too early in the race is likely to drop out toward the end. And the marathoner who paced himself well from beginning to end has a better chance of winning the race.

Build Identity-Based Habits

Old habits die hard. The habits you've kept for the longest will take you longer to break than others. You are also what you eat. For verification of that fact, you only need to look at yourself in the mirror or check your journal notes to see when last you were on a good date with someone. You have been keeping a journal, haven't you? If not, may I remind you once more to do so? I've already provided you with notes on how to proceed with this habit in an earlier chapter.

Breaking bad habits is not as bad as you may think. It's just a question of replacing them with good habits. Journaling is one of those habits. So too, healthy balanced eating (three meals a day, with healthy snacks in between). But if your bad habits are based on who you are as an individual, don't worry. You'll surprise yourself by learning that new, better habits can be part of your identity too.

How Good Habits Lead to Good Results

If you're still in the process of transforming your habitual behavioral patterns, you can look forward to good habits because the results you'll achieve through practicing them are powerful. But be warned, no matter how diligently you apply yourself to this transformation, you need to be patient because good habits take time to get used to. Even so, once your new habits have become a regular part of your daily routine, you'll see how much easier it will become for you to reach new goals.

Not only that, these will be notable goals in your life. Once good habits are part of your life, it becomes easier for you to motivate yourself to achieve those goals. Motivation doesn't operate in a vacuum because the practice of good, healthy habits helps you to see and feel how much easier it becomes to complete tasks that, previously, you felt were arduous. Your regular, daily, habitual behavior places you in a position to review the progress you're making toward achieving these goals.

In fact, one study showed what happens when good habits lead to good results. Researchers monitored a group of people who were trying to form better eating habits. Once those people were able to see and feel the results of their improved eating habits, they were encouraged to prolong it. The researchers' work, as well as the behavior of their subjects, responds to human nature in the sense that we're motivated to prolong good habits once we're able to see and experience the results achieved. At the same time, encouragement can be given to drop bad habits, particularly when you're able to see the potential damage it does to you. Life's good, but it's also simple. After all, you're able to see what healthy protein does to your muscles. You're able to experience what additional levels of carbs do to your energy levels when you're running a marathon.

What is an Identity-Based Habit?

Identity-based habits are habits that are performed as a reflection of who you are as a human being. It's also a reflection of your personal circumstances, as well as the things and people that you are drawn to or surrounded with, whether by choice or even under duress.

Positively speaking, identity-based habits are part of your personality. It doesn't require much effort or motivation for you to pursue these habits. Such habits are performed automatically because they're an innate part of your identity.

Now, if some of the habits that you're practicing are inherently bad for you, will it be possible for you to change them? Of course, it will. But in order to do so, you would definitely have to replace them with good alternatives.

Like taking up a good reading habit (you're reading books, of course) to replace the time you spend on social media and binge-watching TV shows that you aren't even remotely interested in. Like practicing healthy eating habits from morning to evening to replace the junk food cravings you might feel after a long, hard workout at the gym. And like following a new circuit or strength-training routine to replace the excessive reps you can barely manage on the weights floor.

How to Build Good Habits

It may take a while but I strongly believe that you can build new habits that will be beneficial for your self-esteem and personal growth. New habits will help you to become fitter and stronger, both physically and mentally. Don't delay the process of building new habits for yourself, and start working your way through the following steps:

- Begin by writing down what you'd like to do. Try to keep this list as short as possible.

- Work toward fitting these new habits into your daily routine but introduce them in small increments, one day at a time.

- After a few days of practicing, use your journaling time (good habit) to reflect on any progress or setbacks you've experienced.

- As you reflect on any relapses you may have experienced, start training yourself to become better disciplined.

Breaking old, bad habits will always have its challenges. But experiencing the results that your new, healthy habits have produced for you is worth celebrating. So, surround yourself with healthy, positive people who can support you when you're finding it difficult to keep yourself together. And let these same good people be part of your celebrations.

The Four Laws of Habit Change

Changing your habits from bad to good doesn't need to be intimidating. After all, there are only four laws of habit change that need to be observed. They are cue, craving, response, and reward. These laws, making up a four-step pattern, form the backbone of every habit. Unbeknown to you, your brain runs through these steps in the same order, each time you approach a familiar or new habit.

A better understanding of how this process works might be helped if we observe the science of how habits work. To improve our understanding of this process, we also need to break down these fundamental parts. It will help us to understand how the process works, and what could be done to improve it.

Cue

The cue is giving your brain a clue. It is triggering your brain to initiate a behavior. The cue provides your brain with information that hints at a reward. It was an incentive that our prehistoric ancestors could use well because it allowed them to signal the location of primary rewards like food and water, and even sex. But today, our focus seems to have shifted to money, status, praise and approval, love and friendship. Above all, we are always looking for personal satisfaction.

Moreover, this shift in reward incentives has improved our chances of survival. In the meantime, the cue prompts your mind to continuously analyze your surrounding environment in order to locate the rewards you seek. Finally, because your cue is the first sign that you're closer to a reward, you develop a craving for that reward.

Craving

This is the second step of your habit-forming loop. It is the motivation behind every habit you form. If you had no craving for food, you wouldn't bother to get up in the morning to go hunt for food. But you will, no doubt, starve to death, so motivation is always with you, my friend. Here's another way of putting it. If you're a smoker, you're not craving the smoking of the cigarette but you are craving the feeling of relief it provides. You don't crave the action of cooking a meal but you do crave the taste and comfort that each meal provides. You will have many cravings, and no one craving will be the same.

But in essence, as human beings, we are all motivated by the same cues. Finally, cues remain meaningless to you until they are interpreted, and the thoughts, feelings, and emotions you experience will be converted into a craving.

Response

The response is critical because it is the habit you perform. Your habit doesn't need to imply an action, it can just be a thought. Just how intense your response is to your craving, depends on how motivated you are to perform the habit. Your response is also influenced by your ability to perform the habit. Indeed, if cooking a meal is too much trouble for you, you might be inclined to switch your thoughts to ordering a cheeseburger and fries instead. It takes no trouble to do so. But it doesn't do your health any good. Of course, because of its preoccupation with the craving, this warning may never have entered your mind. All it was focused on was enjoying the reward.

It is your response that delivers the reward. It is the end goal of every habit. While the cue notices the reward, and the craving wants the reward, the response obtains the reward. Finally, you will pursue your rewards because they will satisfy you.

Reward

Rewards serve two purposes, namely to satisfy your craving and to teach you which actions are worth remembering. You are motivated by rewards because you know that they will deliver benefits such as satisfying your hunger or thirst or getting into shape to help improve your health and even your dating prospects. Rewards deliver contentment and relief from the craving.

There are lessons to be learned from being rewarded. Your sensory nervous system monitors the actions that satisfy your desires and deliver pleasure. Feelings of pleasure, as well as disappointment, form part of the feedback mechanism that helps your brain to distinguish useful actions from necessary actions. Finally, rewards close the feedback loop and complete the four-step habit cycle.

The feedback loop is an endless cycle that never stops running, even while you're sleeping. The so-called habit loop continuously scans your environment, predicting what will happen next, trying out different responses, and learning from the results they achieve.

All four of the above steps can be broken down further into two phases, namely the problem phase and the solution phase. The problem phase deals with cues and cravings, while the solution phase provides the response and rewards. Whether good or bad, all habit-forming behavior is motivated by the desire to solve a problem. Whether the problems are good or bad, every habit's purpose is to solve the problems you're faced with.

Why Repetition Is the Most Effective Ways to Develop Composure

Here I am talking from personal experience, but I'm also taking into account those that have been driven by their emotions, and have been overwhelmed by them. It will take longer for them to develop forceful, willful habits that work in their best interests.

Repetition is one such good habit that no disciplined, successful sportsman wants to break. To this day, I remain enthralled by the weight training metaphor because it emphasizes in such simple terms how repetition benefits us. So, when you begin to learn how to compose yourself, you'll train yourself at the most basic level. It is routine-driven and inspires confidence because every week that you track your progress, you'll see how well you've improved.

The weight training example is apt because it shows that by lifting weights, one rep after another, you will eventually get strong. You'll also build stamina through anaerobic exercises like road running or cycling. But still, there's something missing from this repetition cycle. While all strength comes from repetition, repetition becomes a cycle easy to repeat when you've applied your mind to the power of repetition. Note the following three benefits of repetition before learning to keep track of your habits:

- Repetition helps you to master your action: After repeating a set of reps or cycles, you're forced into a situation where you're required to reflect on the progress you made and correct errors, if any, made during this process.

- Repetition builds discipline: The process of going through the same routine over and over again may seem tiresome initially but does build discipline for as long as you repeat the routine.

- Repetition builds confidence: Knowing that you've grown better and stronger after completing each cycle is surely a confidence builder.

It can also stimulate you to move out of your comfort zone and take a discerning approach to the new habits you're endeavoring to perfect.

Move Out of Your Comfort Zone and Track Your New Habits

Call me old-fashioned but I'd like to advocate a move away from using social media apps to help track your new habits. At the same time, I cannot prevent you from using online habit trackers. Let me explain why I prefer the good old-fashioned manual pen-and-paper method. It's similar to the journal or diary-keeping process. And because your mind is focused on the paper drafting exercise, it is a cognitive process.

All you need is a calendar to begin with. Use it to cross off each day that you've stayed true to your new routine. This simple tracker provides immediate evidence that you've completed your habit, and as each month passes by, it will present you with renewed signs that you're making progress. Indeed, habit tracking is powerful for the following three reasons:

- Visual cues are created to remind you to act.

- The visual progress chart is a motivating factor. You're always able to see how much progress you're making.

- You take pride in recording your progress at the moment.

Create a Composed Environment

You need to surround yourself with love. You need to disperse with the self-loathing and hate. Your surrounding environment needs to be indicative of the man you want to become. Surround yourself with winners, and say goodbye to all the losers in your life because you're here to show the world that you're a man who can handle all kinds of pressure.

But no matter how strong you think you are, you still can't do it alone. Show me a strong leader who in all honesty and decency, can claim that he did it all by himself. We are who we are because of others.

Identify Yourself as a Man Who Can Handle All Kinds of Pressure

Everything that has been written or read before about keeping yourself together is worth reminding yourself about. After all, like me, you are still on a growth curve, and even if you could presume that you've reached the top of the ladder, there is still room for improvement. Harness yourself well, and you'll never cave under pressure. Ever again.

In the spirit of sticking to good habits, I've compiled a list of habits practiced by those who do well under pressure. While you're still working toward improving your abilities, the following habits are worth reflecting upon:

- **Keep yourself flexible**: Make a note that your best-laid plans should always be subject to change. This may be the case when unforeseen circumstances force you to drop what you're doing and change course. Remember always that mastering the art of working under pressure means that you'll need to keep yourself adaptable to change.

- **Prevent pressure from spiraling out of control**: Through journaling and other self-care practices, you can restrain yourself from caving under pressure.

Whenever you're faced with a high-pressure situation, you need to reflect objectively. Doing so will help prevent you from lapsing into a worrying spiral of overthinking.

- **Practice self-care**: It's worth reminding yourself of this. After compiling a list of daily exercise routines, healthy meal plans, and de-stressing exercises, you can use your habit tracker to make sure that you stick to your self-care routine.

- **Trust the support you've been given**: Bearing in mind that you can't do everything yourself, trust others to assist you whenever they can. Remember, you need to ask for their support, particularly if sociological patterns prevent you from seeing trusted family members and friends on a regular basis. They may not always be able to offer you material support but if you've chosen your friends well, they can offer you emotional support.

- **One step at a time**: While you cannot do everything yourself, you cannot do everything at once. Thriving under pressure is all about dealing with one situation at a time. Understand the task you need to fulfill, and what is required of you, and do not panic. Also, break down each problem into a series of smaller, manageable steps, one step at a time.

You Are the Product of Your Environment

You need to remind yourself that the people and situations you surround yourself with, could shape how you think, feel, and act. So, if the environment you're in is toxic, then you'll need to shift yourself away from this environment. If not that and if you have the strength to do so, start influencing others on how your ideal environment should look. Either way, you may still need to step out of your comfort zone. Humble yourself enough to be associated with people who are better than you. Don't let their superior skills intimidate you. Rather, learn from them.

In other words, surround yourself with winners. It is through honest hard work and perseverance, passion and enthusiasm, integrity, and even humility that they get to be where they are in life. You'll also find that they've already made themselves accountable to others. Under their good example and influence, you can make yourself accountable too, providing yourself with better skills to analyze the environment you find yourself in and remove all weaknesses.

Make Winning Seem Effortless

After months of practice, and after months of trying, soon, you'll become a winner. But if it's going to take longer for you to reach your objectives, don't let the time required disillusion you. Just as long as we keep on practicing, we are all destined to become winners. Keeping your composure while putting in the effort will certainly help. At the same time, giving others the impression that you're already a winner will do you no harm. After all, if they're led to believe that you're a winner, they could be led to have confidence in you and put trust and faith in your abilities.

Don't Let Your Wins Go to Your Head

It is, however, probably a better idea for you to prove your practical worth. Having the gift of the gab is all good and well but when it comes down to the brass tacks, will you really be up to the job? Even small wins along the way toward your stated objective, might not be sufficient to win the hearts and minds of others. More time is needed to convince them.

On the other hand, if you're already on a winning streak, it could become too tempting to get carried away, particularly if you've never experienced that winning sensation before. Personally, I find humility to be the best quality to keep to help keep me grounded. I have experienced what winning does to me. People thought differently of me but it was a false impression that I gave them. Internally, I didn't feel good about this.

Don't let your future success go to your head. When it happens, be humble about what it took for you to become successful, and always remember that humility is a sign of strength, not weakness. Remember to acknowledge the help you received along the way. Express gratitude for the knowledge you acquire.

The Dangers of an Inflated Ego

If you become so successful in life, you might be prompted into thinking that you're invincible. You've been out of the danger zone for a while, and the thought has entered your mind: Nothing can touch me now. I'm good, and I'm going to get better. Things seem to be easier for you than it ever was for you at any stage of your life. While you still work hard to maintain your success, complacency begins to creep into your subconscious thinking. You're in the process of developing an inflated ego. You have entered a danger zone again.

Your inflated ego leads to a distorted perception of reality. The world remains yours for the taking. But when problems arise, and they will, you blame others for them. Overstating your contributions to your success, you've dismissed the efforts made by others. This could be particularly damaging if you're now a leader of men, running your own business, or the captain of your sports team. Don't let this happen to you, my friend. It isn't worth the stress and anxiety that your inflated self-image could cause.

There are two ego barriers that could destroy your ability to remain successful, namely an inability to be introspective, and an over-inflated perception of your self-worth. Thinking that you're better than everyone else could lead to bitter resentment. You become blind to your weaknesses and become cannon fodder for those who've had just about enough of your attitude.

How to Compose Yourself When Winning

When life starts to shine for you, don't give up on the self-development exercises you started practicing to help develop and maintain your composure. No matter how successful in life you are, and no matter how much you keep on winning, you still need to keep yourself composed.

Toward the end of this chapter, I've compiled a list of what I've called masters of composure. As you read through what they've achieved, you should be inspired to emulate their example. One fine example is that of investment guru, Warren Buffett, who to my mind, is the epitome of composure. When markets are down, and others are selling their stocks like hot potatoes, Buffett remains calm.

As a successful trader, Buffett's not about to change his investment strategy. When markets and profits increase exponentially, he won't alter his strategy to take advantage of this trend. He'd much rather buck the trend. He's certainly not a gambler, and would much rather play by the rules he's set for himself. Finally, Buffett observes one of the fundamental rules of successful investing by taking a long-term view of everything he does.

You can apply the investment metaphor to your life too, no matter what you're doing, and no matter how well you're doing it, by focusing only on the goals you've set for yourself. Stick to your plan, and don't deviate from it.

Maintaining the Composed Image

Maintaining your composure throughout your life will remain hard work. But if you've habitually acquired the discipline to maintain it, it should become a flawless exercise. Maintaining your composed image takes work as well. It is all about presentation. Think about it this way: In order to sell a service or product, you still need to look your best. And you have to be on your best behavior, always mindful of what the other person might be thinking. After all, first impressions last.

I'm not advocating that you should always wear a three-piece suit and tie. Doing that is uncomfortable enough, even in the eyes of others. If you've done your homework on what others like, and what makes them comfortable in the room, you will dress and act appropriately. Most importantly, you should still stick with just being yourself. But if, like me, you're at your most relaxed in a pair of jeans and a T-shirt, first consider the occasion before getting carried away with your self-image.

Combat Sports: Lock and Engage

You need to take your mind off the daily pressures of life. You need to preoccupy your mind elsewhere. Spending focused time with things of interest not related to work or family responsibilities is a self-help form of CBT. I take a lot of pride and joy in my reading and writing. At the best of times, it relaxes me. It helps me to compose my thoughts. But when there's too much pressure at certain times of the month, I find it difficult to use this practice as a form of relaxation. After all, whether directly or indirectly, reading is part of my work.

At such times, my mind should be elsewhere. Being at the gym is great but then I'm thinking of the performance and wellbeing of my small team of athletes. So, I need to take my mind still further. Walking, and even running has been good for me but because it's a solitary pursuit, my mind can still be drawn to my work and family affairs. So, what's next for me?

It's time to lock and engage. If boxing or paintball war games are not for you, there are always contact sports like basketball, soccer, or even squash. You're in competition with yourself but you're also in competition with others. What better way is there to take your mind off the daily stresses of life?

Going All in

What does it mean to go all in? It means going for it, even when it's hard, even when you're under pressure to perform. It means willing yourself to take risks, even with the knowledge that there's always the possibility that you might fail. It means having to persevere and not give up. Going all in entails a willingness to try new things when other efforts have failed you.

This clarion call has been popularly applied to the game of poker. Remember James Bond and the scarred villain Le Chiffre from the *Casino Royale* movie? I remember a scene from the movie where Bond asks fellow-agent, Felix Leiter, to cover for him in case he loses. Even so, the suavely dressed Englishman would more than likely still have risked his all if he was left to his own devices. It was in his never-say-die nature. It was never again for him.

Going all in does not, however, suggest that you should throw away all your hard-earned earnings on a poker game. If you lose, you'll have more than a gambling problem to contend with. Play your cards right, keep your cards close to your chest, and you'll have a better than even chance of winning.

Just Do It, Even When It's Hard

You may just find that if whatever you're faced with is not hard, it's probably not worth contemplating. I have found this out from personal experience. To my mind, it's indicative of the fixed mindset being stuck in a rut. Life becomes boring but it's perceptively safer that way. It's a lot better than living on the edge, and having your fingernails chewed to the quick every time you go out to face the world. But it still happens, doesn't it?

No matter how peaceful and free of worry your life may seem to you, there will always be a thief in the night. Hiding away for the rest of your life does you no good. You go nowhere, and you achieve nothing in life. But when life's hard, it becomes better when you've just done whatever's in front of you, no matter how hard it was. You chipped away, never giving up. And when you achieve the results you were hoping for, you feel as though you're on top of the world.

Entertain to Win

Nothing pleases me more than seeing a team playing to win. Of course, you'll agree with me on this, that it's a no-brainer, and it's what you and many other fans pay good money to see. But you see, nothing pleases me more than seeing legendary actor and movie producer, Jack Nicholson and Spike Lee, sitting side by side, beaming from ear to ear, watching their beloved Lakers team go down in a blaze of glory. With just seconds to go before the shooter goes off, and with such a wide margin of points to close, LeBron James and the rest of the team play to entertain.

They may have lost the game. You can tell by the way their huge shoulders sink but internally, they're still feeling good about themselves, knowing full well that they gave their game against formidable opponents their best shot. Nothing pleases me more than seeing a side five or six goals down, with nothing more to play for than pride, never throwing in the towel until the referee's final whistle has finally blown. Men (and women) like these, no matter how many times they lose a game, will still be winners in my eyes. In my eyes, they're still playing to win. They're also entertaining to watch. It is an example for the rest of us to follow.

The Masters of Composure

Of course, the tradition of throwing the towel into the ring in a professional boxing bout, is an entirely different matter. The ringside assistant has no alternative but to do this. His boxer is at risk of suffering a severe and dangerous injury, and the referee will not hesitate to call off the fight. It goes without saying that he'll also act on his own initiative, sensing that the defeated fighter can go no further. But it's interesting to observe that for as long as no such call is made, such fighters will carry on taking blows to the head in the hope that they can find an opening to land a surprise punch. Such is the spirit of never giving up, even when all composure is lost.

But with composure, how much more could be achieved? Let me close this chapter with just a couple more examples of great men who never seemed to lose their composure, even when under pressure.

Warren Buffett

For most of his life, he has been known as the Oracle of Omaha. It's as though he always had a crystal ball in front of him that allowed him to make the right call in the financial markets. But there's more to Warren Buffet's staying power that often goes unnoticed. When others choose to panic, he remains calm. When others choose to sell, he buys. Buffet's ability to compose himself goes further than being able to discipline himself.

One of the things I like about Buffet's personality is that as one of the world's richest billionaires, he still leads a simple, quiet life. He prefers a burger and soda to a gourmet dinner. He drives his own sedan while others are driven in limousines. His dress sense appears to be drab while others dress to the nines. All things being equal, Warren Buffet is a humble man who never takes his life for granted.

Special mention should also go to one of the world's most formidable entrepreneurs, South African-born, Elon Musk, founder of ground-breaking, innovative companies such as PayPal, Tesla, and SpaceX. While Musk's brash, eccentric personality could not have been more different from Buffet's, he is, to my mind, a man who's fully in control of his destiny. Sporadic, outrageous remarks made on his X feed can be taken with a pinch of salt, as far as I'm concerned, and I cannot imagine anyone else performing with the same amount of composure as this 21st-century pioneer has.

Sir Alex Ferguson

Alex Ferguson is known to football fans as, quite possibly, the greatest coach ever. As I wrote in an earlier chapter, he's got many titles to prove this. But for Ferguson, it wasn't always like this. Indeed, his first couple of seasons with Manchester United were precarious, to say the least. There were always rumors that he could be fired at any moment. But no, the club's board members placed their faith in him to deliver the goods. Ferguson could endure the pressure and the early defeats because he had composure.

Jimmy Kimmel

I have to admire one of America's favorite comedians, Jimmy Kimmel. He is a man who appears to take jibes and glares in response to his insinuating humor in his stride. Perhaps Kimmel has had luck on his side. After all, his predecessor as master of ceremonies at the annual Academy

Awards, Chris Rock, fell victim to a man who completely lost it. That said, special mention should go to Robert Downey Jr. who I thought, composed himself rather well when Kimmel continued to taunt him relentlessly at the 2024 awards ceremony while all others in the audience could enjoy a good laugh at the Academy Award winner's expense.

Compared to how the talented actor lived his life in the past, you could even say that Robert Downey Jr. is a real Iron Man. Indeed, keeping your composure at the best of times, and at the worst of times, remains hard work. As I said earlier, it's a full-time job. But given what can be achieved, it is a job well worth keeping.

Conclusion

I would not have told you this story if I didn't believe it was possible. I would not have motivated you to build and develop your self-composure if I did not believe in the results that could be achieved. And yet still, I must take my hat off to you if you've been at the bottom of the food chain. You're no longer there. You've pulled yourself up by the bootstraps and are living to fight another day, figuratively speaking of course, but in the boxing ring, it remains a living reality.

I know this because boxing is a sport I've given my life to. If it weren't for composure, who knows how many more of my boxers could have gone down before the bell. That they endured is due to their own resilience and never-say-die attitude. I might have been their mentor but take no credit for their achievements. Now, let me end *The Art of Composure* by reflecting on some of the highlights of what you've read.

Our first task was to create a better understanding of composure. Doing so, I took pride in sharing with you some of the psychological aspects of composure. This, to my mind, could override some of the misconceptions about composure we've had to deal with. It was also important to reflect on the role composure plays in our lives, learning to appreciate that we can only benefit once we've composed ourselves.

Before turning to strategies to help you develop your composure, I felt that it was necessary to reflect on the harsh reality of a life lacking in composure. At this point, the less said, the better. Rather, let us reflect on what can be achieved. It can begin with something as tremendous as changing your identity. This is a prospect that should not intimidate you. Rather, reflect on the practical, everyday tasks—from mindfulness practices to building discipline—that can also equip you for those high-pressure situations in life when composure starts to sag.

From learning to communicate effectively, to navigating conflict situations, dealing with pressure, solving complex problems, to priming yourself for leadership roles, I took delight in providing you with a rich variety of characters. What could be more rewarding than reading what it takes to be a champion in life? There is, of course, the story of young Charles, previously known as The Pushover. Today, that title no longer applies to him, and sometimes, I wonder how he would compose himself as a mature adult when faced with a hot-headed bully.

All things being equal, we now know that nothing works better than taking a level-headed approach toward dealing with conflict and solving problems. To this end, I introduced a number of strategies, from negotiation tactics to preparation work, that you can apply to your daily life as it stands.

I've touched briefly on the differences between the fixed mindset, and the growth mindset. As its name implies, the latter mindset is a beacon of growth, always willing to learn something new, and even when success has been achieved, to continue growing. As I've said before, there's always room for improvement. The growth mindset also teaches you to remain resilient in the face of adversity. But the fixed mindset threatens you to remain in your comfort zone, venturing no further than the safe walls you've built around yourself. Going no further in life, in other words. What could be worse than that?

Come to think of it, life could get worse. That is not through a lack of trying. In fact, you may have already done your best. You continue to discipline yourself to keep yourself together in the face of challenging everyday situations that could have caused you to overreact previously. No matter how well you've equipped yourself, there will always be new challenges to face, some of them quite unexpected.

The book's last chapter was designed to motivate you to keep on growing, and getting you to believe that all things are possible for you. Throughout this book, I've utilized real-life men to inspire you. I've also used characters lacking in composure to warn you. Talking about leadership was not an afterthought. If I look back at my life, I never anticipated that I would become a leader myself. I didn't even plan for it. And yet still, I became a leader. Given my experience at this level, I felt that it was necessary to talk about leadership to help you anticipate what will be expected of you.

Talking to you has been one of the most rewarding experiences of my life. I have done my duty. No matter how many men read this book, I may never know what they go on to achieve in life. But that's okay because I have every confidence that you will be successful in life, no matter what challenges you are faced with. Keep on training yourself to be composed, my friend, and you *will* be well.

References

Arcement, B. (2019, March 26). *The 6 challenges leaders face.* The Business Journals. https://www.bizjournals.com/bizjournals/how-to/human-resources/2019/03/the-6-challenges-leaders-face.html

Bamford, T. (2012, March 9). *15 greatest team captains in NHL history.* Bleacher Report. https://bleacherreport.com/articles/1096961-15-greatest-team-captains-in-nhl-history

Bates, C. (2020, March 23). *6 strategies for keeping your composure while leading through COVID-19.* FEI. https://www.financialexecutives.org/FEI-Daily/March-2020/6-Strategies-for-Keeping-Your-Composure-While-Lead.aspx#:~:text=Composure%20helps%20people%20make%20a,positive%2C%20can%2Ddo%20spirit.&text=Anxiety%2C%20concern%20and%20frenetic%20energy,stay%20focused%2C%20calm%20and%20productive.

Behnke, C. (2017, May 1). *If it's worth doing it will be hard, if it's not hard, then it's probably not worth doing.* https://medium.com/@chrisbehnke/if-its-worth-doing-it-will-be-hard-if-it-s-not-hard-then-it-s-probably-not-worth-doing-a61474e1cc85

Being assertive: reduce stress, communicate better. (2024, January 20). Mayo Clinic. https://www.mayoclinic.org/healthy-lifestyle/stress-management/in-depth/assertive/art-20044644

Ben. (2024). *The importance of preparation and time management: U2's guide to academic success in 2024.* U2Tuition. https://www.u2tuition.com/resources/time-management#:~:text=Preparation%20allows%20you%20to%20relax,that%20of%20%E2%80%9Ctime%20management%E2%80%9D.

Bindal, S. (2016, April). *6 common myths about mental strength!.* Your DOST. https://yourdost.com/blog/2016/04/myths-about-mental-strength.html?q=/blog/2016/04/myths-about-mental-strength.html&

Blue, K. & Lauer, L. (n.d). *The 3 C's of being a captain.* Association for Applied Sports Psychology. https://appliedsportpsych.org/resources/resources-for-athletes/the-3-c-s-of-being-a-captain/

Borsini, A., et al. (2020). *Food and mood: how do diet and nutrition affect mental wellbeing?.* National Library of Medicine. https://www.ncbi.nlm.nih.gov/pmc/articles/PMC7322666/

Bozza, A. (2009, May 17). Being Eminem. *The Guardian.*https://www.theguardian.com/music/2009/may/17/eminem-urban-music-relapse

Building your resilience. (2020, February 1). American Psychological Association. https://www.apa.org/topics/resilience/building-your-resilience

Bungu. (2016, November 2). *Be humble: don't let success go to your head.* LinedIn. https://www.linkedin.com/pulse/humble-dont-let-success-go-your-head-engineer-knowledge-bungu/

Changing habits. (n.d). University of North Carolina at Chapel Hill. https://learningcenter.unc.edu/tips-and-tools/changing-habits/#:~:text=According%20to%20experts%20with%20Psychology,etched%20into%20our%20neural%20pathways.%E2%80%9D

Cherry, K. (2022, July 25). *How self-monitoring can help you adapt your behavior.* Verywell Mind. https://www.verywellmind.com/what-is-self-monitoring-5179838

Cherry, K. (2023, November 9). *How to improve your self-control.* Verywell Mind. https://www.verywellmind.com/psychology-of-self-control-4177125

Clear, J. (n.d). *How to start new habits that actually stick.* https://jamesclear.com/three-steps-habit-change#:~:text=All%20habits%20proceed%20through%20four,the%20same%20order%20each%20time.

Clear, J. (n.d). *The ultimate habit tracker guide: why and how to track your habits.* https://jamesclear.com/habit-tracker

Cookes-Campbell, A. (2022, April 14). *Contingency planning: 4 steps to prepare for the unexpected.* BetterUp. https://www.betterup.com/blog/contingency-planning

rittenden, J. (2018). What's a guy to do? *Sevenground rules for working with women.* The Discreet Guide. https://www.discreetguide.com/articles/whats-a-guy-to-do-seven-ground-rules-for-working-with-women/

Cuncic, A. (2024, February 12). *7 active listening techniques for better communication.* Verywell Mind. https://www.verywellmind.com/what-is-active-listening-3024343

Dangers of an overinflated ego. (2014, April 17). PeopleFirst. https://www.people1sthr.com/dangers-of-an-overinflated-ego/

Dealing with bullying and workplace conflict: guide for managers. (2022, March 14). CIPD. https://www.cipd.org/en/knowledge/guides/workplace-conflict-people-manager-guide/

Dialectical behavior therapy (DBT). (2022, April 19). Cleveland Clinic. https://my.clevelandclinic.org/health/treatments/22838-dialectical-behavior-therapy-dbt

Doll, K. (2023, April 4). *You are a product of your environment-so make it count.* Shortform. https://www.shortform.com/blog/you-are-a-product-of-your-

environment/#:~:text=(Shortform%20note%3A%20In%20T
he%20Compound,think%2C%20feel%2C%20and%20act.

Edger, M. (2010, September 17). *Wayne Gretzky on the mental game of hockey*. Sports Psychology Today. https://www.sportpsychologytoday.com/sport-psychology-for-athletes/wayne-gretzky/

8 common symptoms of social communication disorder. (2020, December 19). https://www.greatspeech.com/8-common-symptoms-of-social-communication-disorder/#:~:text=Greeting%20Others%20Inappropriately&text=Other%20individuals%20might%20use%20nonsensica l,communication%20disorder%20could%20be%20present.

Emotion regulation. (n.d.). Psychology Today. https://www.psychologytoday.com/za/basics/emotion-regulation

Employees who go the extra mile. (n.d.). Engage Employee. https://www.engageemployee.com/blog/employees-who-go-the-extra-mile#:~:text=Going%20the%20extra%20mile%20is,demons trated%20by%20%27engaged%27%20employees.

Excitement. (n.d.). Personal Synthesis. https://www.personalsynthesis.com/excitement/

Ferguson, R. (2013, December 18). *29 benefits of composure for leaders*. Ferguson Values. https://www.fergusonvalues.com/2013/12/29-benefits-of-composure-for-leaders/

Fey, T. (2024, May 8). *7 signs you're a confident introvert who is happier being alone*. Global English Editing. https://geediting.com/signs-youre-a-confident-introvert-who-is-happier-being-alone/#:~:text=If%20you%20find%20yourself%20relishing,creative%2C%20or%20simply%20at%20peace.

Finkelstein, D. (n.d). *How to avoid getting overwhelmed while setting your goals?*. Tick those boxes. https://tickthoseboxes.com.au/how-to-avoid-getting-overwhelmed-while-setting-your-goals/

Flexner, V. (2023, January 2). *4 leadership qualities business owners should strive for in 2023*. The Story Exchange. https://thestoryexchange.org/4-leadership-qualities-business-owners-should-strive-for-in-2023/?gad_source=1&gclid=CjwKCAjw34qzBhBmEiwAOUQcFoB6-hvugq7QSL715wyRdlWNHcr2HliIsVK6kC1mJubsTHmAbKpl3RoCrTkQAvD_BwE

Foroux, D. (2018, January 22). *All strength comes from repetition*. https://dariusforoux.com/repetition/

Gaines, C. (2022, November 28). *Here are all 3 times Luis Suarez has bitten opponents*. Yahoo. https://uk.sports.yahoo.com/news/3-times-luis-suarez-bitten-211434061.html?guccounter=1&guce_referrer=aHR0cHM6Ly93d3cuZ29vZ2xlLmNvbS5waLw&guce_referrer_sig=AQAAAMYD0Ga7wzsz4aqkasJl149maaf9OKZCQq3v5XOOzADuuNV_qhIEJkVN1Y59Sw8nNrPVxYBaY9scqkgcogqzKvBm-

L_cXyNW4NMobVSQpIKXkwpsGPSQkg4qUqQPK6yzNmK
QaTxMbnuvCBRLxbtAMr3lgybyOVzkAlL1111jUdGv

Ghatak, S. (2023, July 4). *The lessons we learn: lessons from adversity: overcoming challenges and finding strength.* Linkedin. https://www.linkedin.com/pulse/lessons-we-learn-from-adversity-overcoming-challenges-santanu-ghatak/

Gotter, A. (2024, March 15). *Breathing exercises to increase lung capacity.* Healthline. https://www.healthline.com/health/how-to-increase-lung-capacity

Goold, N. (2023, January 20). *Staying calm after making profits.* TitanFx. https://titanfx.com/news/staying-calm-after-making-profits

Guarnaccia, M. (2024, May 1). *Can people change, or do they just lie? Understanding personal growth.* Better Help. https://www.betterhelp.com/advice/behavior/can-people-change-or-do-they-just-lie/

Harris, E. (2023, January 11). *10 habits of people who thrive under pressure.* Truity. https://www.truity.com/blog/10-habits-people-who-thrive-under-pressure

Harry, J. (2022, August 10). *How to manage inner conflict and find wellness.* UT Southwestern Medical Center. https://www.utsouthwestern.edu/about-us/faculty-wellness/archives/thrive/inner-conflict.html

How psychologists help with anxiety disorders. (2023, November 30). American Psychological Association. https://www.apa.org/topics/anxiety/disorders

How to deal with setbacks. (n.d). My MnCareers. https://careerwise.minnstate.edu/mymncareers/advance-career/deal-with-setbacks.html

How to get impulsive behavior under control. (2023, June 7). Talkiatry. https://www.talkiatry.com/blog/impulsive-behavior

How to learn from your mistakes. (n.d). Mind Tools. https://www.mindtools.com/a27yhpa/how-to-learn-from-your-mistakes

How to overcome social anxiety: 8 tips and strategies. (2023, July 18). Calm. https://www.calm.com/blog/how-to-overcome-socia-anxiety

Identity-based habits: how your habits shape your identity (examples). (2021, October 14). Ringoals. https://ringoals.com/identity-based-habits/#:~:text=Identity%2Dbased%20habits%20are%20the,behind%20him%20in%20the%20supermarket.

Kim, J. (2024, April 30). *Why slowing down is essential for your growth.* Psychology Today. https://www.psychologytoday.com/intl/blog/the-angry-therapist/202404/why-slowing-down-is-essential-for-your-growth#:~:text=When%20we%20slow%20down%2C%20we,our%20values%2C%20and%20our%20aspirations.

King, J. (2013, March 14). *Why "practice makes perfect.".* CMC. https://motivationandchange.com/why-practice-makes-perfect/#:~:text=Deliberately%20practicing%20new%20behavior%20has,habit%20of%20replacing%20old%20habits!

Krastev, S. (n.d). *Fixed mindset.* The Decision Lab. https://thedecisionlab.com/reference-guide/psychology/fixed-mindset

Llopis, G. (2014, January 20). *7 ways leaders maintain their composure in difficult times.* Forbes. https://www.forbes.com/sites/glennllopis/2014/01/20/7-ways-leaders-maintain-their-composure-in-difficult-times/?sh=6ccfc31d2157

Makridis, C. (2018, April 20). *The power of repetition.* Medium. https://medium.com/writers-guild/the-power-of-repetition-2932767759eb

Martins, J. (2024, January 30). *How to lead by example, according to one Asana leader.* Asana. https://asana.com/resources/lead-by-example

Matejko, S. (2022, October 11). *Social awkwardness: signs and how to overcome it.* PsychCentral. https://psychcentral.com/health/socially-awkward#:~:text=Social%20awkwardness%20is%20when%20you,new%20people%2C%20can%20be%20awkward.

Mead, S. (n.d). *What to do when you lose your composure.* Center for Management and Organization Effectiveness.

https://cmoe.com/blog/what-to-do-when-you-lose-your-composure/

Muñoz, P. (2024, April 22). *How to project your voice (without yelling).* WikiHow. https://www.wikihow.com/Project-Your-Voice-(Without-Yelling)#:~:text=Hissing%3A%20Take%20a%20deep%20breath,time%20than%20the%20hissing%20version.

Ngui, A. (2023, November 14). *Weak leadership: how bad leaders undermine success.* IDT World. https://itdworld.com/blog/leadership/weak-leadership/#:~:text=When%20leaders%20are%20weak%2C%20unclear,collaboration%2C%20further%20impacting%20overall%20productivity.

Nunez, K. (2020, August 10). *The benefits of progressive muscle relaxation and how to do it.* Healthline. https://www.healthline.com/health/progressive-muscle-relaxation

Pacor, G. (2021, June 21). *Are you a 'pushover' at work?.* Aigroup. https://www.aigroup.com.au/resourcecentre/resource-centre-blogs/hr-blogs/are-you-a-pushover-at-work/

Pederson, T. (2022, April 28). *What are triggers, and how do they form?.* Psych Central. https://psychcentral.com/lib/what-is-a-trigger

Peek, S. (2023, November 16). 5 reasons why teamwork is crucial for worplace success.

Perry, E. (2022, March 30). *Self-esteem isn't everything, but these 5 tips can give you a boost.* BetterUp. https://www.betterup.com/blog/how-to-improve-self-esteem

Personality. (n.d). American Psychological Association. https://www.apa.org/topics/personality#:~:text=Personalit y%20refers%20to%20the%20enduring,%2C%20abilities%2 C%20and%20emotional%20patterns.

Prior, E. (n.d). *Increasing and maintaining emotional control under pressure.* Believe Perform. https://members.believeperform.com/increasing-and-maintaining-emotional-control-under-pressure/#:~:text=Emotion%20regulation%20is%20present ed%20as,level%20(Tamir%2C%202011).

Pushover. (n.d). Vocabulary. https://www.vocabulary.com/dictionary/pushover#:~:text= A%20pushover%20is%20a%20person,anyone%20what%20t hey%20ask%20for.

Raeburn, A. (2024, January 7). *Want to be a better leader? Try being vulnerable.* Asana. https://asana.com/resources/vulnerable-leadership

Rainjitananda, A. (2023, July 13). *Replacing bad habits with meditation: a journey of transformation.* Path of Bliss. https://www.pathofbliss.com/blog/13227313?gad_source=1 &gclid=CjwKCAjw9cCyBhBzEiwAJTUWNYwo9AQFgwRJIfT 2vUNMidIMuO6phdiY6_rKRhaFO_yLu_7uhxbeMBoCtpoQ AvD_BwE

Raypole, C. (2023, February 9). *How to become the boss of your emotions.* Healthline. https://www.healthline.com/health/how-to-control-your-emotions

Resilience. (n.d). American Psychological Association. https://www.apa.org/topics/resilience

Rice, A. (2021, September 13). H*ow to challenge negative self-talk.* PsychCentral. https://psychcentral.com/lib/challenging-negative-self-talk

Robinson, L., et al. (2024, February 5). *Conflict resolution skills.* HelpGuide. https://www.helpguide.org/articles/relationships-communication/conflict-resolution-skills.htm

Segal, J. et al (2024, May 8). *Body language and nonverbal communication.* HelpGuide. https://www.helpguide.org/articles/relationships-communication/nonverbal-communication.htm

Self-esteem. (2022). Mind. https://www.mind.org.uk/information-support/types-of-mental-health-problems/self-esteem/tips-to-improve-your-self-esteem/

Simon, G. (2022, March 23). *Hot headed and cold hearted characters.* Character Matters. https://www.drgeorgesimon.com/hot-headed-and-cold-hearted-characters/#:~:text=Hot%20Headed%20Characters%20in%

20Relationships&text=They%27re%20easily%20irritated%2
0and,behave%20better%20the%20next%20time.

Social anxiety disorder (social phobia). (2022, October 4).
Cleveland   Clinic.
https://my.clevelandclinic.org/health/diseases/22709-
social-anxiety

Smith, J. (2024, January 10). *Why do Gen Z and millennial
men have lower testosterone levels?.* Medichecks.
https://www.medichecks.com/blogs/testosterone/why-do-
gen-z-and-millennial-men-have-lower-
testosterone#:~:text=Obesity%20and%20sedentary%20lifes
tyles,lower%20testosterone%20levels%20%5B11%5D.

Stottler, W. (n.d). *What is problem solving and why is it
important.*   Kepner-Tregoe.   https://kepner-
tregoe.com/blogs/what-is-problem-solving-and-why-is-it-
important/#:~:text=Problem%2Dsolving%20helps%20us%2
0understand,in%20a%20continually%20changing%20envir
onment.

Stress. (2023, February 21). World Health Organization.
https://www.who.int/news-room/questions-and-
answers/item/stress#:~:text=Stress%20can%20be%20defin
ed%20as,experiences%20stress%20to%20some%20degree.

Stress.   (n.d).   Anxiety   UK.
https://www.anxietyuk.org.uk/anxiety-
type/stress/#:~:text=Internal%20stressors%20are%20the%
20sources,low%20self%20esteem%20and%20apprehension
s.

The 4 types of stress. (n.d). TELUS Health. https://healthlibrary.telus.com/en/individuals-families/the-4-types-of-stress

The mark of a master strategist. (2017, April 13). Liros Group. https://lirosgroup.com/blog/the-mark-of-a-master-strategist

The power of composure: a guide to unleashing your leadership potential. (n.d). Corporate Classic Inc. https://www.corporateclassinc.com/the-power-of-composure-a-guide-to-unleashing-your-leadership-potential/#:~:text=Composure%20is%20a%20leadership%20trait,and%20inspire%20confidence%20in%20others.

The power of good habits. (n.d). Mindtools. https://www.mindtools.com/asjk493/the-power-of-good-habits

Tips for ADHD impulse control in adults. (2023, January 18). The ADHD Center. https://www.adhdcentre.co.uk/tips-for-adhd-impulse-control-in-adults/

Townsend, S. (2022, April 22). *Are you a solutionist?.* Futerra. https://wearefuterra.com/blog/are-you-a-solutionist

Tredgold, G. (2016, October 10). *Secret to success: aim high, start small, and keep going.* Inc. https://www.inc.com/gordon-tredgold/secret-to-success-aim-high-start-small-and-keep-going.html

Twin, A. (2024, February 26). *Outsourcing: how it works in business, with examples.* Investopedia. https://www.investopedia.com/terms/o/outsourcing.asp#:~:text=lower%2Dcost%20olocations.-
,What%20Is%20Outsourcing%3F,costs%20on%20labor%2C %20among%20others.

Vidotto, A. (n.d). *How to remain composed while handling conflict.* Her Business. https://herbusiness.com/blog/remain-composed-handling-conflict/

Waak, J. (n.d). *The power of community: 6 reasons we need each other.* Tiny Buddha. https://tinybuddha.com/blog/6-reasons-we-need-each-other-the-power-of-community/

Ways to feel more comfortable in social situations. (n.d). The Social Skills Center. https://socialskillscenter.com/ways-to-feel-more-comfortable-in-social-situations/

What are the characteristics of a winner?. (n.d). Allpro Dad. https://www.allprodad.com/what-are-the-characteristics-of-a-winner/

What are the most effective strategies for finding common ground in a conflict?. (n.d). LinkedIn. https://www.linkedin.com/advice/0/what-most-effective-strategies-finding

What is a growth mindset and how to develop it in 9 steps. (2023, August 16). Persona. https://www.personatalent.com/development/how-to-cultivate-a-growth-mindset

What is cognitive behavioral therapy?. American Psychological Association. https://www.apa.org/ptsd-guideline/patients-and-families/cognitive-behavioral

What is inhibitory control?. (n.d). Foothills Academy. https://www.foothillsacademy.org/community/articles/inhibitory-control-adhd#:~:text=Inhibitory%20control%20is%20a%20core,to%20think%20before%20we%20react.

What's the difference between stress and anxiety?. (2022, February 14). American Psychological Association. https://www.apa.org/topics/stress/anxiety-difference#:~:text=People%20under%20stress%20experience%20mental,the%20absence%20of%20a%20stressor.

Wick, D. (2022, March 14). *To change your behavior, change your identity.* Strategic Discipline. https://strategicdiscipline.positioningsystems.com/blog-0/to-change-your-behavior-change-your-identity

Wooll, M. (2021, November 29). *Can't think straight? How to achieve mental clarity.* BetterUp. https://www.betterup.com/blog/mental-clarity#What

Wooll, M. (2022, February 24). *How to build the discipline of self-discipline.* BetterUp. https://www.betterup.com/blog/how-to-be-disciplined